AMP QReads™

Level F

D1475988

PEARSON

AGS Globe

Shoreview, Minnesota

AMP™ *QReads*™ is based upon the instructional routine developed by **Elfrieda (Freddy) H. Hiebert** (Ph.D., University of Wisconsin—Madison). Professor Hiebert is Adjunct Professor at the University of California, Berkeley and has been a classroom teacher, university-based teacher, and educator for over 35 years. She has published over 130 research articles and chapters in journals and books on how instruction and materials influence reading acquisition. Professor Hiebert's TExT model for accessible texts has been used to develop widely-used reading programs, including *QuickReads*® and *QuickReads*® *Technology* (Pearson Learning Group).

The publisher wishes to thank the following educators for their helpful comments during the review process for *AMP*™ *QReads*™. Their assistance has been invaluable:

Shelley Al-Khatib, Teacher, Life Skills, Chippewa Middle School, North Oaks, MN; **Ann Ertl,** ESL Department Lead, Champlin Park High School, Champlin, MN; **Dr. Kathleen Sullivan,** Supervisor, Reading Services Center, Omaha Public Schools, Omaha, NE; **Ryan E. Summers,** Teacher, English, Neelsville Middle School, Germantown, MD.

Acknowledgments appear on page 176, which constitutes an extension of this copyright page.

Copyright © 2008 by Pearson Education, Inc., publishing as Pearson AGS Globe, Shoreview, Minnesota 55126. All rights reserved. Printed in the United States of America. This publication is protected by copyright, and permission should be obtained from the publisher prior to any prohibited reproduction, storage in a retrieval system, or transmission in any form or by any means, electronic, mechanical, photocopying, recording, or likewise. For information regarding permission(s), write to: Rights and Permissions Department, One Lake Street, Upper Saddle River, New Jersey 07458.

Pearson AGS Globe™, AMP™, QReads™, and QuickReads® are trademarks, in the U.S. and/or in other countries, of Pearson Education, Inc. or its affiliate(s).

ISBN-13: 978-0-7854-6307-8
ISBN-10:   0-7854-6307-0

1 2 3 4 5 6 7 8 9 10   11 10 09 08 07

1-800-992-0244
www.agsglobe.com

CONTENTS

Social Studies

Literature and Language

Science

Arts and Culture

Welcome to QReads™!

Please follow these steps for each page of readings:

FIRST READ

1. Read the Fast Facts and think about what you might already know about the topic. Look for two words that are new or difficult. Draw a line under these words.

2. Read the page aloud or silently to yourself. Always include the title at the top of the same page. Take as much time as you need.

3. Find the first page in Building Connections. Write some words or phrases there to help you remember what is important.

SECOND READ

1. Listen and read along silently with your teacher or the audio track.

2. Use the target rate of 1 minute when listening and reading along.

3. Ask yourself, what is one thing to remember? Answer the Key Notes question to help find what is important.

THIRD READ

1. Now, try to read as much of the page as you can within 1 minute.

2. Read silently as you are timed for 1 minute. Read aloud with a partner or your teacher. Circle the last word you read at the end of 1 minute.

3. Write down the number of words you read on the page. Review in your mind what is important to remember.

4. Complete the questions or other reading given by your teacher.

Speeches That Inspire

Speeches can inspire an audience.

Fast Facts

- Patrick Henry gave his famous speech on March 23, 1775.

- Another speech Henry gave included the statement "United we stand, divided we fall."

- Henry was born in 1736 and died in 1799.

The Power of Speech

Speeches can affect people deeply. The words in a speech can calm, anger, or inspire the people in an audience. However, the way in which the words are said can also affect people.[37]

Today, speeches can be recorded with video cameras and other machines. People who were not in the audience when the[57] speech was delivered can hear and see the speech. They can be calmed, angered, or inspired, just as the first audience was.[79]

A written copy of a speech can affect people, too. Many famous speeches were made before video cameras were[98] invented. In 1775, Patrick Henry made a speech that ended with the words "Give me liberty or give me death." Even today,[120] Patrick Henry's speech still inspires Americans to fight for their liberty.[131]

KEY NOTES

The Power of Speech
How can speeches affect people?

_____

_____

Speeches That Inspire

President Franklin D. Roosevelt delivered
a famous speech to Congress in 1941.

Fast Facts

- In the Pearl Harbor attack in 1941, 2,388 lives were lost.

- Franklin D. Roosevelt was elected president four times—more than any other president.

- In another speech, Roosevelt said, "The only thing we have to fear is fear itself."

A Day of Infamy

On December 7, 1941, Pearl Harbor, in Hawaii, was attacked by Japan. The surprise attack killed many people and destroyed[24] many ships. People feared that the United States mainland would be attacked, just like Hawaii had been.[41]

The day after the attack, President Franklin D. Roosevelt spoke to Congress, describing December 7 as "a date which will[61] live in infamy." He said that we, as Americans, "will not only defend ourselves . . . but will make very certain that this . . . shall never endanger us again."[87]

President Roosevelt said that Americans must work together to prevent future attacks. The speech helped to calm people's[105] fears, but it also inspired them to act. Throughout the war that followed, Roosevelt's Day of Infamy speech reminded Americans that they must work together to win the war.[134]

KEY NOTES

A Day of Infamy

What did President Roosevelt tell Americans in his speech?

_____

_____

Speeches That Inspire

President John F. Kennedy delivered his inaugural address to a large crowd in Washington, DC.

Fast Facts

- John F. Kennedy was the youngest person to be elected president.

- In another speech, Kennedy said, "Race has no place in American life or law."

- The 1960 election debates between Kennedy and Richard Nixon were the first debates on TV.

A Call to Service

American presidents begin a new term by giving a speech called an inaugural address. In 1961, when John F. Kennedy[24] became president, four countries had nuclear bombs, and many people were afraid of the damage nuclear bombs could cause.[43]

In his inaugural address, President Kennedy asked people to work on their shared problems, not their differences. He[61] challenged Americans to "ask not what your country can do for you—ask what you can do for your country." President Kennedy[83] also challenged people around the world to "ask not what America will do for you, but what together we can do for the freedom of man."[109]

President Kennedy's inaugural address inspired people to work for freedom and human rights. He said that working together would make people safe—and free.[133]

KEY NOTES

A Call to Service   What did President Kennedy ask the people of the United States and the world to do?

_____

_____

Speeches That Inspire

Dr. Martin Luther King, Jr., spoke at the Lincoln Memorial in 1963.

Fast Facts

- In 1964, Dr. Martin Luther King, Jr. won the Nobel Peace Prize for his work in civil rights.

- Dr. King believed that equal rights should be gained without violence.

- In another part of Dr. King's speech, he said, "Let freedom ring" for all people.

I Have a Dream

On a hot day in 1963, more than 250,000 people gathered at the Lincoln Memorial in Washington, D.C., to hear [24] Dr. Martin Luther King, Jr. speak. Standing in front of the Lincoln Memorial, Dr. King said that he wanted equal rights [45] for all people. Dr. King reminded people that African Americans did not have the same rights that white Americans had. [65]

Dr. King repeated the phrase "I have a dream" to describe his hopes for the future, including his dream that his "four [87] children will one day live in a nation where they will not be judged by the color of their skin but by the content of their [113] character." Dr. King's "I have a dream" speech continues to inspire people to dream—and to work—for human rights. [133]

KEY NOTES
I Have a Dream
What did Dr. King say he wanted in the speech "I Have a Dream"?
_____
_____

Speeches That Inspire

The Power of Speech

1. Another good name for "The Power of Speech" is _____

    a. "Give Me Liberty."
    b. "How Speeches Affect People."
    c. "Recorded Speeches."
    d. "Famous Speeches."

2. Some speeches are powerful because they can _____

    a. change the way people think.
    b. tell people how to change their lives.
    c. cause people to act in a certain way.
    d. all of the above

3. How might seeing a person give a speech be different from watching a recorded speech?

_____

_____

_____

A Day of Infamy

1. "A Day of Infamy" is MAINLY about _____

    a. what happened in World War II.
    b. why President Roosevelt wrote speeches.
    c. why Japan attacked Pearl Harbor.
    d. President Roosevelt's speech after the Pearl Harbor attack.

2. President Roosevelt gave his Day of Infamy speech
because _____

    a. the United States had been attacked.

    b. the United States had attacked Japan.

    c. Japan had attacked England.

    d. the war had just ended.

3. How did Roosevelt's speech help Americans during the war?

_____

_____

_____

A Call to Service

1. An inaugural address is a speech that _____

    a. tells about how people should fight a war.

    b. American presidents give when they begin a new term.

    c. tells people why they should vote for someone.

    d. American presidents give at the end of their term.

2. In his speech, President Kennedy challenged people around the
world to _____

    a. ask what America could do for them.

    b. work together to change laws in the United States.

    c. inspire their leaders to solve their problems.

    d. ask what they could do to help themselves and others.

3. What did President Kennedy mean when he said, "Ask not what your country can do for you—ask what you can do for your country"?

_____

_____

_____

I Have a Dream

1. What was the main idea of Dr. King's speech?

    a. that everyone should be able to dream
    b. that all people should have equal rights
    c. that Dr. King dreamed of being president
    d. that people gathered to hear Dr. King speak

2. What was Dr. King's dream?

_____

_____

_____

3. Why was the Lincoln Memorial a good place for Dr. King to give this speech?

_____

_____

_____

challenged	Hawaii	inaugural	infamy
inspire	memorial	audience	video

1. Choose the word from the word box above that best matches each definition. Write the word on the line below.

A. _____ asked people to do something difficult

B. _____ to cause someone to want to do something

C. _____ marking the beginning of something

D. _____ something created to remember or celebrate a person or event

E. _____ a recording of pictures and the sounds that go with them

F. _____ a group that listens to or watches a speaker or event

G. _____ a state in the United States that lies in the Pacific Ocean

H. _____ the fame that results from an evil or shocking act

2. Fill in the blanks in the sentences below. Choose the word from the word box that completes each sentence.

A. The president's _____ address told how he wanted to help the country.

B. We recorded the game with our new _____ camera.

C. The speech will _____ everyone to help others.

D. The speaker _____ the people to work for civil rights.

E. Pearl Harbor, in _____, was attacked by Japan.

F. The surprise attack was remembered as an act of _____.

G. The _____ reminded the country of the people who had fought and died in the war.

H. The _____ listened to the speaker talk about times when people had few rights.

Speeches That Inspire

1. Use the chart to help you remember what you read. Draw a line from each quotation to the person who said it.

Who Said What?

A. "Give me liberty or give me death."

President John F. Kennedy

B. "a date which will live in infamy"

Dr. Martin Luther King, Jr.

C. "Ask not what your country can do for you—ask what you can do for your country."

Patrick Henry

D. "I have a dream."

President Franklin D. Roosevelt

2. How did two of the speeches in this topic inspire people?

_____

_____

_____

_____

3. Why do you think the speakers in this topic wanted to give speeches that inspired people?

_____

_____

_____

_____

4. If you were asked to give a speech to a large group of people, what would you want to inspire them to do? Why?

_____

_____

_____

_____

Purchasing Power

Every country has money, or currency, in the form of paper or coins.

Fast Facts

- The government prints about 37 million bills each day, with a value of about $696 million.

- In 1969, the government stopped printing $500, $1,000, $5,000, and $10,000 bills.

- The largest value printed by the U.S. government was the $100,000 bill.

The Value of Money

A $100 bill and a $1 bill use the same kind of paper and ink. The paper used for both bills also has the same value, and[31] both bills cost the same amount to print. However, $100 bills and $1 bills have different values. It takes more work to earn a[55] $100 bill than a $1 bill. A $100 bill can buy more than a $1 bill can buy.[73]

The word *currency* describes the paper money and coins that are "current" in a country. Before the 1930s, countries[92] needed to have an amount of gold that equaled the amount of currency they printed. Gold is no longer needed to back up the[116] currency that countries print. However, if a country prints too much currency, other countries may value it less.[134]

KEY NOTES

The Value of Money

What does the word *currency* mean?

_____

_____

Purchasing Power

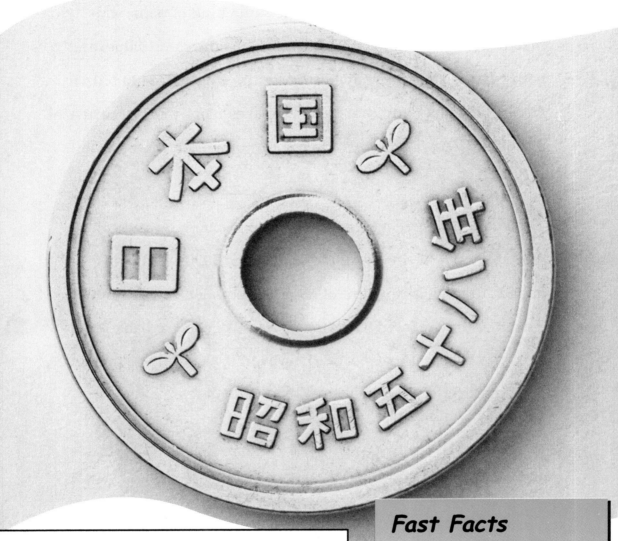

This Japanese coin is circulated in yen.

Fast Facts

- A long time ago, people did not use money. Instead, they got things by trading.

- The first coins may have been made during the 600s B.C.

- Today, more than 180 different kinds of money are used throughout the world.

Dollars, Pesos, and Yen

Each country's government controls the value of the money it circulates. In the United States, the unit of money we circulate[25] is the dollar. Mexico circulates its currency in pesos, and Japan circulates its currency in yen. When people visit other countries[46] or do business around the world, they must exchange their country's money for the money of the country they visit or do business in.[70]

The value of one country's currency compared to the value of another country's currency is called the exchange rate.[89] The exchange rate is the amount of money a person receives for exchanging one country's currency for another country's[108] currency. Exchange rates change from day to day. In the first part of 2006, one U.S. dollar was worth 117 yen or nearly 11 pesos.[133]

KEY NOTES

Dollars, Pesos, and Yen

What does *circulate* mean in this passage?

_____

_____

Purchasing Power

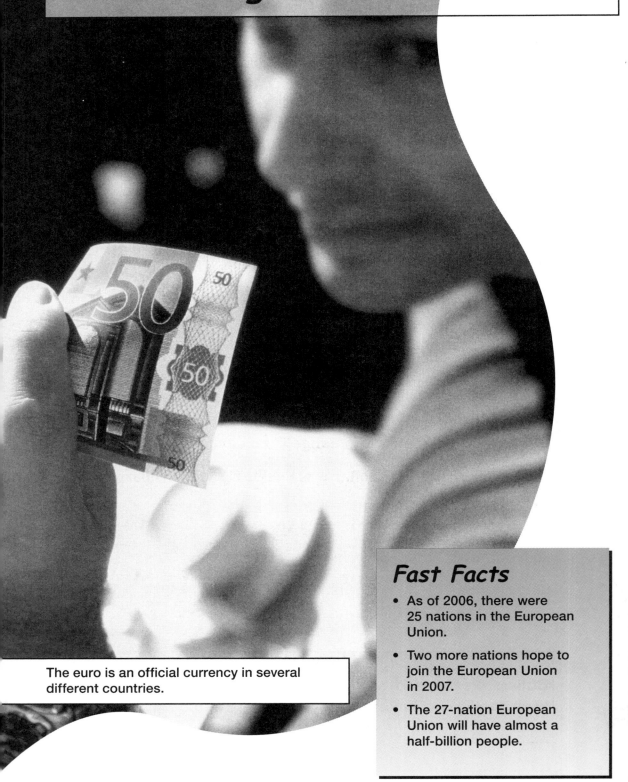

The euro is an official currency in several different countries.

Fast Facts

- As of 2006, there were 25 nations in the European Union.

- Two more nations hope to join the European Union in 2007.

- The 27-nation European Union will have almost a half-billion people.

A Common Currency

The countries in Europe, such as Germany, France, and Italy, are close together. However, until 2002, these three[21] countries used different currencies. Travelers exchanged German marks for French francs, or French francs for Italian lira.[38]

In 2002, Germany, France, Italy, and nine other European countries began to use the same currency. This new currency[57] was called the euro. Euro banknotes, or paper money, look the same in all European Union countries. Euro coins, though,[77] look the same on only one side. Each country uses its own design on the other side.[94]

The single currency has made it easier to travel and do business in the European Union. As of 2005, only three[115] countries in the European Union did not use the euro. Instead, each country continued to use its own currency.[134]

KEY NOTES

A Common Currency

How did the euro change the way people travel in Europe?

_____

_____

Purchasing Power

Consumers in the United States like the convenience of credit cards.

Fast Facts

- The word *credit* comes from the Latin word meaning "trust."

- Financial institutions give people credit ratings, which help determine how much credit a person can have.

- It is estimated that U.S. consumers have an average of nine credit cards.

Credit Cards

In 1950, people in the United States had a new way to purchase things—credit cards. Today, many people use credit[23] cards to purchase goods. To get a credit card, people apply to a bank or other financial institution. If their application is[45] accepted, they sign a legal agreement that lists the institution's rules for using the card.[60]

The institution pays for the goods or services a person purchases with the credit card. Then, the person pays the[80] institution back. The institution charges interest, or extra money, for bills the person does not pay right away. Also, there is often a fee for using the credit card.[109]

Credit cards are convenient, but they can also be costly. The interest on unpaid bills can make things cost much more than their original price.[134]

KEY NOTES

Credit Cards

What or who pays for a purchase when a credit card is used?

_____

_____

Purchasing Power

The Value of Money

1. "The Value of Money" is MAINLY about _____

    a. how much money is printed in other countries.
    b. why all countries use the same currency.
    c. how much money is worth.
    d. why people use money.

2. What could happen if a country printed too much money?

    a. The country would exchange it for gold.
    b. People would use other countries' currency.
    c. The government would not use it.
    d. Other countries would value it less.

3. What is *currency*?

_____

_____

_____

Dollars, Pesos, and Yen

1. People need to exchange their money in other countries
because _____

    a. different countries use different currencies.
    b. other countries do not use currency.
    c. pesos can only be used in Japan.
    d. money only has value in the country that printed it.

2. Who controls the value of the money a country circulates?

   a. the people in the country
   b. the government of the country
   c. the exchange rate
   d. the government of the United States

3. What is the exchange rate?

_____

_____

_____

A Common Currency

1. What is the euro?

   a. the name of the European Union
   b. the currency that replaced the dollar
   c. the exchange rate in Europe
   d. the currency used in the European Union

2. Coins used by European Union nations _____

   a. have different values in each country.
   b. look the same on one side but different on the other side.
   c. have different names in each country.
   d. look exactly the same in every country.

3. How has the euro made it easier to travel and do business in the European Union?

_____

_____

_____

Credit Cards

1. What is listed in a legal agreement for a credit card?

    a. the institution's rules for using the card
    b. the amount of money a person must pay for goods
    c. the stores that will accept the credit card
    d. the kinds of cards the financial institution sells

2. How are credit-card purchases paid for?

_____

_____

_____

3. What is a possible problem with using credit cards?

_____

_____

_____

| value | currency | circulate | exchange |
| euro | application | institution | purchase |

1. Choose the word from the word box above that best matches each definition. Write the word on the line below.

A. _____ a large group of people working together for the same purpose, such as in a school or library

B. _____ the paper money and coins that are used in a country

C. _____ how much something is worth

D. _____ a written form that is used to ask for something

E. _____ to buy something

F. _____ to give one thing and receive another thing in return

G. _____ the name of a unit of money that is used in many European Union countries

H. _____ to move something from person to person or place to place

2. Fill in the blanks in the sentences below. Choose the word from the word box that completes each sentence.

A. I had to _____ the shirt for another one because I'd bought the wrong size.

B. My old shoes had no _____ because they had holes.

C. The financial _____ agreed to give Sandy a loan.

D. Last month, Paul sent an _____ for a credit card.

E. The _____ of the United States is called dollars and cents.

F. Jenny had to _____ a new jacket because her old one was torn.

G. Money will _____ through the hands of many people.

H. The _____ has made it easy for people to buy things in different European countries.

Purchasing Power

The Value of Money

_____

_____

_____

_____

Dollars, Pesos, and Yen

_____

_____

_____

_____

Purchasing Power

A Common Currency

_____

_____

_____

_____

Credit Cards

_____

_____

_____

_____

2. What are three facts you learned about money in this topic?

_____

_____

_____

_____

3. Are credit cards a good way to buy things? Explain your answer.

_____

_____

_____

_____

4. Suppose there was another passage in this topic. Do you think it would be about banks or about traveling in Europe? Why?

_____

_____

_____

_____

Ancient Greece

The people of ancient Greece gathered in markets like the one in this picture.

Fast Facts

- The Golden Age of Greece took place in the 400s B.C.

- Greek civilization reached its height during a period called the Golden Age of Greece.

- Athens and Sparta were the most important city-states of ancient Greece.

The Ideas of Ancient Greece

Greece is a country in southern Europe. It is where the Olympics began, more than 2,500 years ago. Ancient Greece is[26] often called "the birthplace of the Western world." That is because the ideas of the ancient Greeks influenced the people of Europe and North America.[51]

In ancient Greece, city-states were the centers of civilization. City-states had their own governments and ruled[69] the land around them. The ancient Greek city-states also had the first democratic governments. Until that time, no[88] government had been chosen by its people. In fact, the word *democracy* comes from the Greek words for *people* and *rule*.[109]

Today, many nations have democratic governments, and people from around the world enter the Olympics. The ideas of ancient Greece are still very much alive.[134]

KEY NOTES

The Ideas of Ancient Greece
Describe the city-state government of ancient Greece.

_____

_____

Ancient Greece

This statue shows the Greek god Atlas carrying the world on his back.

Fast Facts

- The gods that Atlas fought against were the gods of Mount Olympus.

- The Atlas Mountains, in northwest Africa, are named for Atlas.

- Atlas's brother was the god who gave people fire.

Greek Myths

The ancient Greeks believed that gods and goddesses made and ruled the world. Greek writers and poets wrote about these[22] gods and goddesses. Today, their writings are known by the Greek word *myth*, which means "story." Myths helped the Greeks explain why some things happened in their world.[50]

One character in Greek myths was Atlas. Atlas was a god who took part in a battle against other gods. Because his group[73] lost the battle, Atlas was punished by having to carry the world on his back. Today, some people are described as being "as[96] strong as Atlas" or "having the burdens of Atlas." *Atlas* is also the name for a book of maps. Many other words in English, such as *giant* and *fate*, come from characters in Greek myths.[131]

KEY NOTES

Greek Myths
What is a myth?

_____

_____

Ancient Greece

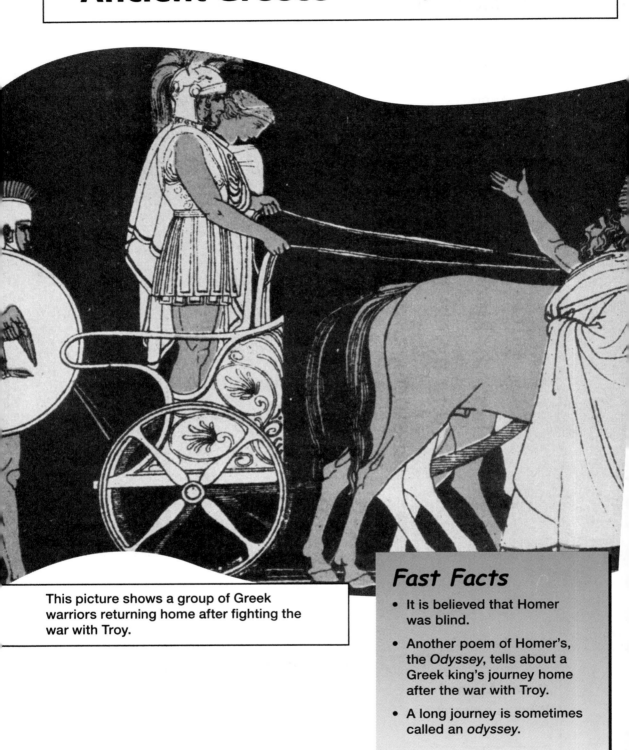

This picture shows a group of Greek warriors returning home after fighting the war with Troy.

Fast Facts

- It is believed that Homer was blind.

- Another poem of Homer's, the *Odyssey*, tells about a Greek king's journey home after the war with Troy.

- A long journey is sometimes called an *odyssey*.

Greek Classics

The literature of the ancient Greeks and Romans is often called the classics. Classics are stories that are read long after[23] they are written and are used as models for writing that comes later. Homer was the most famous ancient Greek writer. One of his long poems is a classic called the *Iliad*.[55]

Before Homer's time, the Greeks fought a ten-year war with the people of the city of Troy. The Greeks finally captured Troy[78] by using a clever trick. The *Iliad* tells about the war with Troy and the disasters that happened to a warrior during the last year of the war.[106]

Homer's poems are so famous that their titles are often used to describe certain events. A series of disasters, for example, is sometimes called an *iliad*.[132]

KEY NOTES

Greek Classics
Who was Homer?

_____

_____

Ancient Greece

Athletes today compete in Olympic Games, which were begun by the ancient Greeks.

Fast Facts

- The ancient Greeks measured time in olympiads, which were the four-year periods between games.

- The first 13 Olympic Games had only one event—a 210-yard race.

- Wrestling and other contests were added to the games in 708 B.C.

Olympic Athletes

The ancient Greeks greatly valued athletics, or skill and strength in sports. Training to be an athlete began when children were as young as seven years old.[29]

Every four years, people from all over ancient Greece gathered to watch athletes compete. The games were held in[48] Olympia, a place named after Mount Olympus, which was where the ancient Greeks believed their most important gods lived.[67] The word *Olympics* came from the name *Olympus*. The Olympic Games were so important to the ancient Greeks that wars were[88] stopped during the month before the games were held. This allowed athletes and visitors to travel safely to the games.[108]

The Greeks treated their Olympic athletes with great respect. Athletes who won their games were believed to be favored by the gods.[130]

KEY NOTES

Olympic Athletes
How do we know the ancient Greeks valued athletics?

_____

_____

Ancient Greece

The Ideas of Ancient Greece

1. Ancient Greece is often called _____

    a. "the birthplace of the Western world."
    b. "the birthplace of the Eastern world."
    c. "the beginning of all civilization."
    d. "the beginning of sports."

2. Greece was the first nation to have _____

    a. gods and goddesses.
    b. democratic governments.
    c. governments like those in Europe.
    d. cities and states.

3. In what ways are the ideas of ancient Greece still alive today?

_____

_____

_____

Greek Myths

1. What did the ancient Greeks believe their gods and goddesses did?

    a. They made and ruled the world.
    b. They wrote stories about things they did.
    c. They created books of maps.
    d. They became characters in myths.

2. What happened to Atlas in the Greek myth?

_____

_____

_____

3. What do you think it means to be "as strong as Atlas"? Explain your answer.

_____

_____

_____

Greek Classics

1. What are the Greek classics?

    a. stories that were quickly forgotten

    b. stories that tell about wars fought in Troy

    c. stories that tell about ancient Greek disasters

    d. stories that are still read long after they were written

2. The _Iliad_ tells about _____

    a. a Greek king's journey home after a war.

    b. a war and the disasters of a Greek warrior.

    c. how the Greeks lost the war with Troy.

    d. how the Greeks built a great city.

3. What is another good title for this passage? Explain your answer.

_____

_____

_____

Olympic Athletes

1. What are athletics?

    a. sports that are played in teams
    b. skill and strength in sports
    c. sports that are not for children
    d. athletes who compete against each other

2. How did the ancient Greeks feel about sports? What facts in this passage tell you this?

_____

_____

_____

3. Why do you think the Olympic Games were held near Mount Olympus?

_____

_____

_____

athlete	classic	democracy	goddesses
myth	*Iliad*	Olympics	compete

1. Choose the word from the word box above that best matches each definition. Write the word on the line below.

A. _____ a story about ancient gods and goddesses that explains why some things happened

B. _____ to play a game with someone and try to win

C. _____ ancient Greek games that featured sports

D. _____ a person who is trained in sports or games

E. _____ a story that is still read long after it was written

F. _____ a kind of government in which the people choose their leaders

G. _____ a long poem about the Greek war with Troy

H. _____ women with great powers who created and ruled parts of the world

2. Fill in the blanks in the sentences below. Choose the word from the word box that completes each sentence.

A. In a _____, people vote for their leaders.

B. The _____ tells stories about a war that was fought by the ancient Greeks.

C. An ancient Greek _____ tells how gods made the world.

D. Reading _____ stories can help you learn to create characters and plots.

E. If you want to become an _____, you have to practice your sport every day.

F. The ancient Greeks believed that _____ could use their great powers to help people.

G. Our team won every game, so we could _____ in the playoffs.

H. Every four years, people all over the world watch the _____.

47

Ancient Greece

1. Use the idea web to help you remember what you read. In each box, write the main idea of that passage.

**The Ideas of
Ancient Greece**

_____

_____

_____

_____

Greek Myths

_____

_____

_____

**Ancient
Greece**

Greek Classics

_____

_____

_____

_____

Olympic Athletes

_____

_____

_____

_____

2. Describe three things that were important to the ancient Greeks.

_____

_____

_____

_____

3. What are two things the ancient Greeks created that exist today?

_____

_____

_____

_____

4. Suppose there was another passage in this topic. Would you expect it to be about ancient Greek schools or about life in Greece today? Explain your answer.

_____

_____

_____

_____

Myths

Myths like Atlas gave answers to questions about the world.

- The Greeks believed that their divinities lived on Mount Olympus.

- The Norse believed that their dead warriors went to a great hall in the sky.

- The ancient Greeks thought of the Sun as a burning carriage being driven across the sky.

What Are Myths?

People have always wanted to know why things happen. Where does the Sun go at night? What causes thunder? How was the world created?[27]

Today, we use science to answer questions like these. Long ago, people found answers in stories called myths. The Norse[47] people believed that a god made thunder with a great hammer. The Egyptians believed that the world was created from a huge body of water.[72]

Many myths are about gods, or divinities. Divinities have powers far beyond what people have, yet in many myths they[92] act like people. They have the same emotions as people and make the same mistakes as people.[109]

Ancient myths are part of our world today. When people talk about someone with a golden touch or opening a box full[131] of trouble, they're talking about things that happen in Greek myths.[142]

KEY NOTES

What Are Myths?
What might you find in a myth?

_____

_____

Myths

One artist showed the Roman god Janus as having two faces.

Fast Facts

- The Roman god of gates and doors had two faces.

- The Roman god of fire had a workshop under a volcano.

- One Roman hero killed two snakes with his hands when he was a baby.

Roman Myths

The study of myths is called mythology. Roman mythology tells stories about ancient Roman divinities and Roman history.[20]

One myth tells how the city of Rome was started. According to this story, there were twin brothers whose mother was a[42] human and whose father was the Roman war god Mars. As babies, the twins were put into a basket that was left floating[65] on a river. A wolf found the basket and saved the twins. When the twins were grown, they decided to build a city at the place where the wolf found them.[96]

The Romans took many of their gods from the Greeks. The chief Roman god, Jupiter, was like the chief Greek god,[117] Zeus. Like Zeus, Jupiter controlled thunder. Another important Roman divinity was Jupiter's wife, Hera, a divinity who was the goddess of women and childbirth.[141]

KEY NOTES

Roman Myths
What is Roman mythology?

_____

_____

Myths

In Egyptian myths, the crocodile was considered divine.

Fast Facts

- Ancient Egyptians sometimes put jewels on crocodiles.

- Ancient Egyptians had different gods for the different positions of the Sun.

- Ancient Egyptians believed that gods protected dead people's lungs, liver, and stomach.

Egyptian Myths

The ancient Egyptians believed that before the world was created, there was nothing but a huge ocean. When a god[22] rose from the water and found that he had no place to stand, he created a hill. Then, he created more gods, who were his[47] children. One day they disappeared, and the god was very upset. When his children finally returned, he cried with joy. As his tears landed on the ground, the tears became people.[78]

After this, the god created crocodiles, other animals, plants, and other living things. In Egyptian mythology, some[95] animals are considered divine. The Egyptians regarded cats and crocodiles as divine.[107]

The sky was a goddess called Nut. She was often shown as a cow standing over Earth. Each morning, she gave birth to the Sun. Each evening, Nut swallowed the Sun, leaving people in darkness.[142]

KEY NOTES

Egyptian Myths

How did the ancient Egyptians believe the world was created?

_____

_____

Myths

This painting shows Pandora, a Greek myth.

Fast Facts

- Athena was the goddess of wisdom and of war.

- Poseidon was the god of earthquakes and of the sea.

- Aphrodite was the goddess of love.

Greek Myths

Some ancient Greek myths are part of the English language today. You may have heard the names of some people from these myths.[25]

The gods gave Pandora, who was said to be the first woman, a box that held many troubles. Pandora was told to never open[49] the box, but she was very curious. One day she lifted the lid and all of the world's troubles flew out. Today, "a Pandora's box"[74] means "something full of trouble." Opening a Pandora's box means releasing the trouble inside.[88]

Another Greek myth tells of Midas, a king who wanted to be rich. When a god granted him a wish, he asked that everything[112] he touched turn to gold. Midas got his wish, but he had a problem—even his food turned to gold. Today, "having the Midas touch" means being successful at everything you do.[144]

KEY NOTES

Greek Myths

Where do you hear the names from ancient Greek myths today?

_____

_____

Myths

What Are Myths?

1. A long time ago, people used myths to _____

  a. give them scientific answers to questions.
  b. explore space.
  c. explain why things happened.
  d. grant themselves wishes.

2. How did Viking myths explain thunder?

  a. A god made thunder from a huge body of water.
  b. A god made thunder with a great hammer.
  c. A god made thunder with a golden touch.
  d. A god made thunder using a box full of trouble.

3. Today, how do we answer questions like "What causes thunder?"

  _____

  _____

  _____

Roman Myths

1. According to Roman mythology, the city of Rome was started
  by _____

  a. the god who controlled lightning.
  b. two brothers who found a wolf in a river.
  c. the goddess of ancient Greece.
  d. two brothers who were saved by a wolf.

2. What are Roman myths about?

_____

_____

_____

3. What god was Jupiter like? How were these two gods alike?

_____

_____

_____

Egyptian Myths

1. According to Egyptian mythology, people were created when
_____

    a. a god's tears landed on the ground.
    b. Egyptians put jewels on crocodiles.
    c. cats became divine.
    d. Nut gave birth to the Sun.

2. The ancient Egyptians believed that night was caused by _____

    a. crocodiles eating the Sun.
    b. Nut swallowing the Sun.
    c. a god standing on a hill.
    d. a god rising from the ocean.

3. In this passage, _divine_ means _____

_____

_____

_____

Greek Myths

1. Who was Pandora?

    a. an evil goddess
    b. a goddess who liked to argue
    c. a goddess who was curious
    d. a goddess who liked myths

2. Why does "having the Midas touch" mean being successful at everything you do?

_____

_____

_____

3. What does it mean to "open Pandora's box"?

_____

_____

_____

myths	divinities	mythology	Zeus
crocodiles	divine	Pandora	Midas

1. Choose the word from the word box above that best matches each definition. Write the word on the line below.

   A. _____ the study of myths

   B. _____ a woman in a Greek myth who opened a box and let trouble into the world

   C. _____ stories told by people to explain why things happen

   D. _____ the chief Greek god

   E. _____ gods and goddesses

   F. _____ large animals with thick skin and long bodies that live in water

   G. _____ having to do with the gods

   H. _____ a king in a Greek myth who turned everything he touched to gold

2. Fill in the blanks in the sentences below. Choose the word from the word box that completes each sentence.

   A. The Greeks believed that _____ let evil into the world by opening a box.

   B. Lisa is so successful that people say she has the _____ touch.

   C. Many myths tell of the _____, or gods and goddesses, of the ancient world.

   D. _____ is the study of stories told by people to explain why things happen.

   E. _____ are animals that live in Egypt today.

   F. The ancient Egyptians believed that cats were _____.

   G. The leader of the Greek gods was named _____.

   H. Lee's favorite _____ are the stories that explain how the stars came to be.

61

Myths

1. Use the idea web to help you remember what you read. In each box, write the main idea of that reading.

What Are Myths?

_____

_____

_____

_____

Roman Myths

_____

_____

_____

_____

Myths

Egyptian Myths

_____

_____

_____

_____

Greek Myths

_____

_____

_____

_____

2. Compare two myths from different cultures that were described in this topic.

_____

_____

_____

_____

3. Why do you think myths existed in ancient cultures?

_____

_____

_____

_____

4. How do people today use science to answer the questions ancient people answered with myths?

_____

_____

_____

_____

All About Advertising

Advertising tells people about services and products.

Fast Facts

- In the United States, more than $200 billion is spent on advertising each year.

- New York City is the center of the U.S. advertising industry.

- There are about 6,000 ad agencies in the United States. About one-third of them are in New York City.

What Is Advertising?

Advertising is a way to tell people about companies, products, services, or ideas. Businesses use ads to sell products[22] and services. People use ads to sell houses, cars, and other things.[34]

Political parties and candidates run ad campaigns to get votes. Groups and organizations run ad campaigns to tell people[53] about a cause or to influence how people think or act on an issue. For example, environmental groups use ads to encourage people[76] to protect the environment. The United States government advertises to encourage people to join the armed forces.[93]

The United States has the largest advertising industry in the world. Ads are important to the communications industry[111] because that's how newspapers, magazines, TV stations, and radio stations earn much of their money. Companies pay[128] for advertising space in newspapers and magazines and for advertising time on television and radio.[143]

KEY NOTES

What Is Advertising?
Who uses advertising?

_____

_____

All About Advertising

Travel magazines are one form of advertising media.

Fast Facts

- Most television commercials are 30 seconds long.

- Newspapers often use almost half of their space for advertising.

- Game and toy companies use about 90 percent of their advertising budget for television ads.

Forms of Advertising

Advertising reaches people through diverse forms of communication called media. Common advertising media in the[18] United States include television, radio, newspapers, magazines, and the Internet.[28]

Television commercials help advertisers reach diverse audiences because most people watch television. Radio helps[42] advertisers reach people who are away from home or who are doing things at home, like exercising.[59]

Newspaper and magazine ads are called print advertising. Because magazines attract certain readers, companies that make[75] CDs advertise in music magazines. Also, sporting goods stores advertise in sports magazines.[88]

The newest form of advertising is Internet advertising. Some companies advertise on the Internet on a Web site. Some[107] companies also advertise on the Internet with pop-up ads on other Web sites.[120]

The next time you buy something, think about where you heard about it. There's a good chance it was through advertising.[141]

KEY NOTES

Forms of Advertising
What are three forms of advertising?

_____

_____

All About Advertising

Endorsements by famous people get an audience's attention.

Fast Facts

- As early as 3000 B.C., people used signs to advertise stores.

- In ancient times, people used symbols to advertise their goods.

- In 2005, a 30-second TV ad broadcast during the Super Bowl cost more than $2 million.

Smart Advertising

To be effective, ads have to attract people's attention. One way to attract attention is to have a famous person in the[24] ad. After all, if your favorite movie star or athlete were in an ad, you'd probably pay attention. This kind of advertising is called[48] an endorsement. Endorsements are effective because they link a company or product with someone many people respect.[65]

Another way for ads to attract attention is through sponsoring a television or radio program. Sponsors are people or[84] companies that pay part of a program's costs. Many people have favorite shows that they tune into, so sponsors know they will have an audience for their ads.[112]

Advertisers spend a lot of time thinking about the people to choose for product endorsements, the programs to sponsor, and[132] the shows to advertise on. Making the right decision is smart advertising.[144]

KEY NOTES

Smart Advertising

What is smart advertising?

_____

_____

All About Advertising

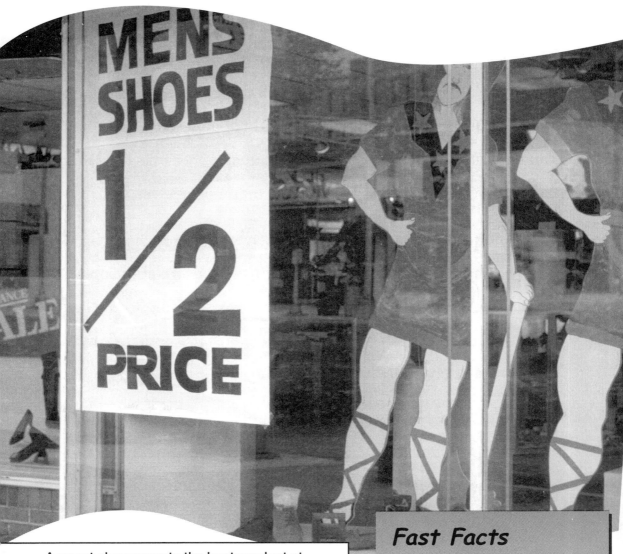

A smart shopper gets the best product at the best price.

Fast Facts

- The first printed advertisement in English appeared in 1472.

- Early ads in the United States and England did not always tell the truth about products.

- Some foods advertised as being low in fat have almost as many calories as foods that are not labeled low-fat.

Advertising and You

Some advertising is deceptive. It manipulates people into spending too much money or buying things they don't need.[21] It could manipulate people into eating food that is not healthful. Some deceptive ads also don't tell the truth about a product or make promises that are later broken.[50]

There are laws against deceptive advertising, but your best protection is to think for yourself. Before you believe what an[70] ad says, ask yourself a few questions about the product. Do you really need new shoes? Do you need those shoes at that exact[94] price? Can you buy other shoes that are just as good for less money?[108]

The purpose of advertising is to make people buy things. Being a smart shopper means only buying the things you want and need, and getting the best product at the best price.[140]

KEY NOTES

Advertising and You

How can ads manipulate people?

_____

_____

All About Advertising

What Is Advertising?

1. The purpose of advertising is _____

    a. to help newspapers and magazines earn money.
    b. to tell people about a product, company, service, or idea.
    c. to encourage people to campaign for their ideas.
    d. to help people protect the environment.

2. In this passage, *campaign* means _____

    a. knowing what things to buy.
    b. an advertising business.
    c. political parties and candidates.
    d. a group of ads that tell about a product or idea.

3. Describe three ways ads are used.

_____

_____

_____

Forms of Advertising

1. Which of the following are common advertising media in the United States?

    a. television and the Internet
    b. commercials and radio
    c. radio and pop-up ads
    d. the Internet and music stores

2. What kind of magazine would be a good place to advertise for a company that sells sneakers?

_____

_____

_____

3. How do companies advertise on the Internet?

_____

_____

_____

Smart Advertising

1. To be effective, an ad must _____

    a. make people ask questions about a product.
    b. sponsor television and radio programs.
    c. attract people's attention.
    d. use a person most people respect.

2. Endorsements are effective because _____

    a. advertisers pay famous people a lot of money for them.
    b. famous people use a lot of the product they advertise.
    c. people know that advertisers tell the truth about a product.
    d. most people pay attention to someone famous.

3. Why might a company want to sponsor a TV show?

_____

_____

_____

Advertising and You

1. How are some ads deceptive?

    a. They appear on television or radio.
    b. They don't tell the truth about a product.
    c. They tell the truth about what they advertise.
    d. They encourage people to buy things.

2. Why is it important to think before you buy a product?

_____

_____

_____

3. What does it mean to be a smart shopper?

_____

_____

_____

sponsor	campaigns	deceptive	diverse
endorsement	encourage	Internet	manipulate

1. Choose the word from the word box above that best matches each definition. Write the word on the line below.

A. _____ a network that links computers around the world

B. _____ a group of ads that tell about a product or idea

C. _____ a person or group that pays for a project or activity

D. _____ not telling the truth

E. _____ to control someone by unfair means

F. _____ a message that encourages people to try a product

G. _____ different from others

H. _____ to try to get someone to do something

2. Fill in the blanks in the sentences below. Choose the word from the word box that completes each sentence.

A. The star's _____ helped sell a lot of cell phones.

B. Some advertisements try to _____ people into buying a product and don't tell the truth.

C. During the election, all of the candidates ran ad _____ to get votes.

D. The cereal company will _____ the children's show because children eat a lot of cereal.

E. People should be careful when they read ads because some advertising is _____.

F. Television commercials advertise _____ products that appeal to many different people.

G. An environmental group might run an ad to _____ people to save whales.

H. More and more people have begun to buy things advertised on the _____.

All About Advertising

1. Use the idea web to help you remember what you read. In each box, write two important facts from each passage.

What Is Advertising?

_____
_____
_____
_____

Forms of Advertising

_____
_____
_____
_____

All About Advertising

Smart Advertising

_____
_____
_____
_____

Advertising and You

_____
_____
_____
_____

2. Describe three ways that companies advertise their products.

_____

_____

_____

_____

3. Why do companies advertise their products?

_____

_____

_____

_____

4. List three questions you could ask yourself before you decide to buy something you've seen advertised.

_____

_____

_____

_____

Careers in Language

Writing and editing a newspaper can be fun.

Fast Facts

- In 2004, about 320,000 people in the United States worked as writers or editors.

- More than one-third of these people were self-employed.

- A college degree is needed for most writer or editor positions.

Writing and Editing

Many people have careers in language. Two popular language careers are writing and editing. Writers work on[20] many different types of materials. They create books, magazine articles, newspaper stories, and ads. They also create content for Web sites and scripts for films and TV shows.[48]

Some editors determine what ideas or articles will appear in magazines or books. They assign articles or book ideas to[68] writers, then they determine if the writer's work meets their needs. Other editors work with writers as they write and help them revise their work.[93]

Most readers think they are reading only a writer's words. However, they are also reading the work of an editor who has[115] worked with the writer to make sure the writer's ideas are presented clearly. People who enjoy working with language might consider a career in writing or editing.[142]

KEY NOTES

Writing and Editing
Describe what writers and editors do.

_____

_____

Careers in Language

Translation puts words into another language.

Fast Facts

- In 2004, about 31,000 people in the United States worked as translators.

- In 2005, the average salary for U.S. government translators was $72,000.

- United Nations translators are required to know at least three official U.N. languages.

Translating

Suppose the leaders of two countries are meeting, and neither one speaks the other's language. When they[18] communicate with each other, they need an interpreter who can translate their words into their own language.[35]

Translating is the process of putting words into another language. Translators' careers involve reading books, articles,[51] and scientific and political papers, and changing the words into another language. Translating is especially important in helping countries understand and do business with one another.[77]

Translation that happens while people talk is called interpreting. Interpreting is very important in places like the[94] United Nations, where people from many different countries gather. When someone speaks at the United Nations, people who[112] don't understand that language can hear a translation through headphones. In that way, with only a few seconds' delay, people[132] can quickly discuss and solve problems that arise around the world.[143]

KEY NOTES

Translating
What do translators do?

_____

_____

Careers in Language

Good communication skills are needed to teach English.

Fast Facts

- Jobs for English teachers may be found around the world.

- The highest-paying jobs for English teachers are in Asia.

- People who teach English in other countries are paid in the currency of that country, not in U.S. dollars.

Teaching English

Being an English teacher requires several skills, but the most important is that the person must be able to communicate[22] with others. In college, people who want to become English teachers study English literature, grammar, writing, and education.[40]

Some English teachers specialize, or focus on one area of teaching. One specialty in the United States is teaching English[60] as a Second Language, or ESL. ESL teachers help people learn to speak, read, and write English. They teach students English sounds and words, and how to use English grammar.[90]

Today, people around the world are learning English. That is because many companies do business in several[107] countries and need to communicate easily. In addition, some jobs, such as flying an airplane, require that people speak[126] English. As people travel and do business in more countries, the demand for English teachers grows.[142]

KEY NOTES

Teaching English
What does ESL mean?

_____

_____

Careers in Language

A speech therapist finds ways for people to communicate better.

Fast Facts

- In 2004, there were about 96,000 speech therapists in the United States.

- The study of speech and speech problems is more than 2,000 years old.

- About 6 percent of the people in the United States have a speech disorder.

Speech Therapy

One career in language has to do with helping people with language problems. Speech therapists help people who have[21] speech and language disorders. Some of these disorders make it difficult for people to communicate with others.[38]

Some people are born with a condition that leads to a speech disorder. Others develop speech disorders during[56] childhood. Speech disorders can also be caused by diseases or by accidents.[68]

First, speech therapists find the cause of the problem. Then, they figure out the best way to help the person. There[89] are many different kinds of jobs for speech therapists. Speech therapists work in schools, laboratories, hospitals, and speech[107] centers. In a way, speech therapists are like doctors. People go to them with problems, and speech therapists find a way to help them either solve their problem or find a way to make it better.[143]

KEY NOTES
Speech Therapy What is a speech therapist?

Careers in Language

Writing and Editing

1. Why are writing and editing considered to be careers in language?

    a. Both involve writing books and magazines.
    b. Both involve working with words.
    c. Both involve programming Web sites.
    d. all of the above

2. What does *determine* mean in this passage?

    a. to assign magazine articles
    b. to decide on something
    c. to change someone's ideas
    d. to revise someone's work

3. How do writers and editors work together?

_____

_____

_____

Translating

1. What do translators do? _____

    a. They put words into another language.
    b. They make sure everyone speaks clearly.
    c. They help people speak each other's language.
    d. They teach people how to speak English.

2. Translation that happens while people talk is called _____

    a. conversing.
    b. meeting.
    c. interpreting.
    d. talking.

3. Why is interpreting important at the United Nations?

_____

_____

_____

Teaching English

1. What do ESL teachers do?

_____

_____

_____

2. In this passage, *specialize* means _____

    a. to teach ESL.
    b. to do something very well.
    c. to focus on an area of study.
    d. to speak more than one language.

3. Many people are learning English today because they want to _____

    a. teach English as a Second Language.
    b. read literature in English.
    c. visit the United States.
    d. communicate with others around the world.

Speech Therapy

1. What do speech therapists do?

    a. speak for people with language disorders
    b. translate people's words from one language to another
    c. teach people how to read and speak English
    d. help people who have speech and language disorders

2. How can speech disorders affect people?

_____

_____

_____

3. What do speech therapists do to help people?

_____

_____

_____

career	determine	interpreter	specialize
translate	ESL	therapists	disorders

1. Choose the word from the word box above that best matches each definition. Write the word on the line below.

A. _____ to put words into another language

B. _____ to make a decision on how something should be done

C. _____ English as a Second Language

D. _____ people trained in ways to treat problems

E. _____ someone who puts words into another language as people speak

F. _____ a job that a person does for a long time

G. _____ problems that make it difficult to do things

H. _____ to focus on one area of study

2. Fill in the blanks in the sentences below. Choose the word from the word box that completes each sentence.

A. Speech _____ are trained to help people with language problems.

B. The president asked for an _____ who could speak Chinese.

C. Because she was able to _____ what the problem was, she fixed it quickly.

D. Zach went to a doctor for help with his vision _____.

E. James wanted to help people learn English, so he became an _____ teacher.

F. Rita liked math so much that she decided on a _____ as a math teacher.

G. Luis can _____ the newspaper and tell his mother what is happening in town.

H. Elsa wanted to _____ as a writer for science magazines.

Careers in Language

1. Use the idea web to help you remember what you read. In each box, write the main idea of that passage.

Writing and Editing

_____

_____

_____

_____

Translating

_____

_____

_____

_____

Careers in Language

Teaching English

_____

_____

_____

_____

Speech Therapy

_____

_____

_____

_____

2. How do people in three of the careers in this topic help others communicate?

_____

_____

_____

_____

3. Describe how two of the careers in this topic are different.

_____

_____

_____

_____

4. What would you need to study to work in two of these careers?

_____

_____

_____

_____

The Human Nervous System

Waving your arms is a voluntary response.

Fast Facts

- Almost all animals, except very simple creatures, have some kind of nervous system.

- The brain and the spinal cord together are called the central nervous system.

- The brain makes up about 2 percent of a human adult's weight.

What Does the Nervous System Do?

Although your body's systems work together, each one has a special job. The job of the nervous system is to manage the other systems.[30]

Your nervous system is made up of your brain, spinal cord, and nerves. Your brain is the control center of your body. Your[53] spinal cord joins your brain to your nerves. Your nerves receive information from inside and outside your body and carry it to[75] your brain. They also carry information from your brain to your muscles so that you can respond.[92]

Your body has two types of responses. One is a conscious response. You think before making conscious responses,[110] like answering a question. The other type of response is an unconscious response. You do not think before making[129] unconscious responses. Jerking your hand away from a flame is an unconscious response. Your muscles respond *before* your brain tells you the flame is hot.[154]

KEY NOTES

What Does the Nervous System Do?

What is your brain's job in your nervous system?

_____

_____

The Human Nervous System

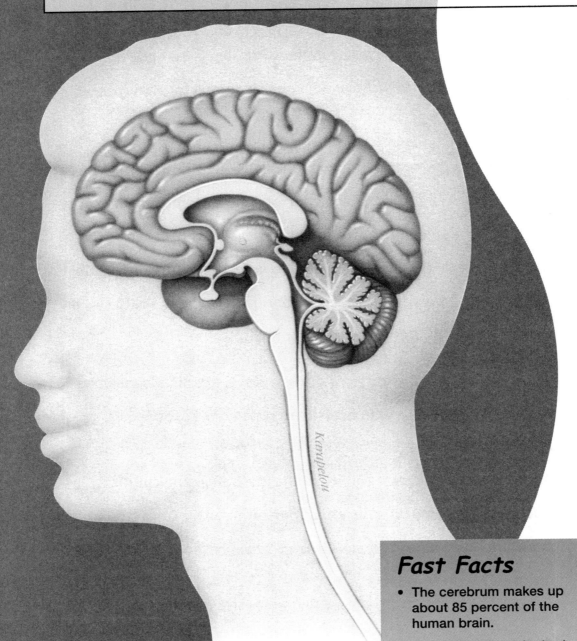

This drawing shows the human brain's cerebrum, cerebellum, and brainstem.

Fast Facts

- The cerebrum makes up about 85 percent of the human brain.

- The right side of the brain controls the left side of the body.

- The left side of the brain controls the right side of the body.

94

The Control Center

The human brain, which weighs about 3 pounds, is not the largest brain on Earth. However, it is the largest when it is compared to the size of the body it is in.[36]

The human brain is also the most complex brain on Earth. It thinks about what is going on around it, and it plans what to[61] do in response. Thinking is a complex process. It allows humans to decide how to respond to things. It allows humans to change[84] themselves and the world around them. It also lets humans create things.[96]

The three main parts of the brain are the cerebrum, the cerebellum, and the brainstem. Thinking and learning take[115] place in the cerebrum. The cerebrum also stores memories. The cerebellum controls muscle movement. It also controls[132] balance, keeping the body steady and stable. The brainstem manages basic life jobs, such as breathing and blood pressure.[151]

KEY NOTES

The Control Center
What does the human brain do?

_____

_____

The Human Nervous System

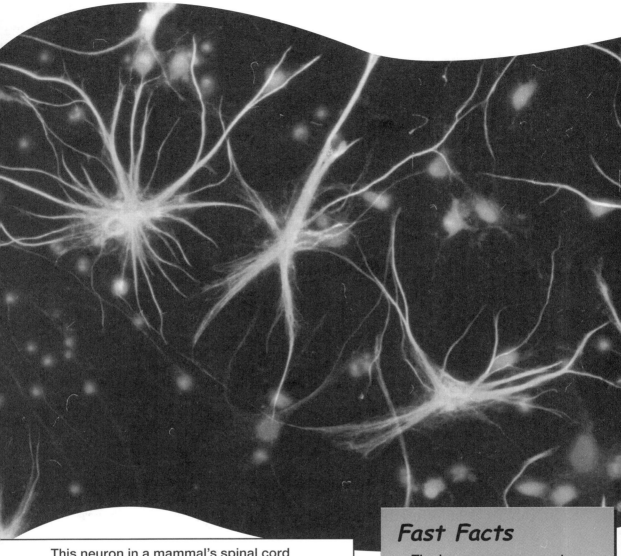

This neuron in a mammal's spinal cord
(in center of photo) is very thin.

Fast Facts

- The human nervous system has billions of neurons.

- The cell part of a neuron is about 1/1000 of an inch wide.

- One neuron can make contact with as many as 1,000 other neurons.

Sending Messages

Nerves are made up of cells called neurons. There are two kinds of neurons: sensory neurons and motor neurons. Sensory[22] neurons send information from the senses to the brain, telling the brain what is happening. For example, they tell the brain[43] that the hand has just touched something sharp or the eye has just seen something big. Motor neurons send messages from the[65] brain to the muscles, telling the muscles how to respond to the information.[78]

Neurons are different sizes and shapes. They can range in size from a fraction of an inch to about 3 feet in length. Most neurons look like an insect with thin legs and a long tail.[114]

A neuron's "legs" pick up information in the form of electrical signals. The signals travel through the neuron to its[134] "tail," where they jump to the next neuron. Some signals can travel very quickly—at about 250 miles per hour.[154]

KEY NOTES

Sending Messages
What are the two kinds of neurons?

_____

_____

The Human Nervous System

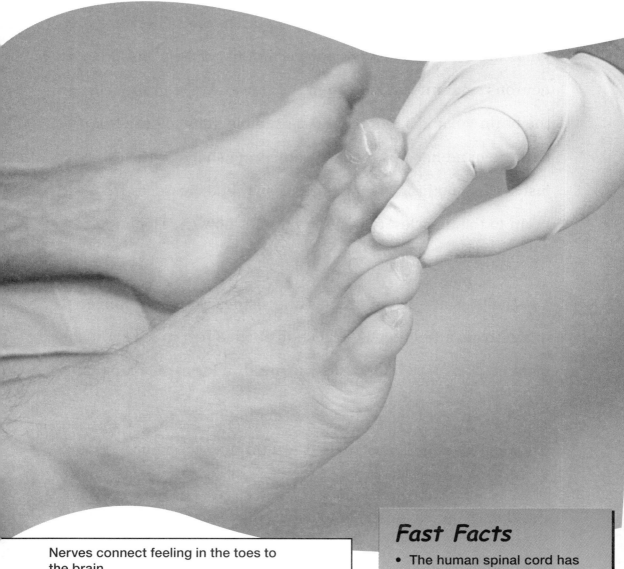

Nerves connect feeling in the toes to the brain.

Fast Facts

- The human spinal cord has 31 pairs of nerves.

- The human backbone has 33 sections.

- In the United States, about 11,000 people injure their spinal cord each year.

The Super-Highway

The human nervous system is like a super-highway that runs through the body. The spinal cord, which is made up[24] of bundles of nerves, starts at the brain and extends about 18 inches down the back, through a hollow part of the backbone.[47] All along the spinal cord, nerves branch off and extend to different parts of the body, connecting the body to the brain.[69]

The nerves at the bottom of the spinal cord connect the legs to the brain. If the bottom of the spinal cord is damaged,[93] messages cannot go from the legs to the brain, and a person could be paralyzed. People who are paralyzed might be unable to walk at all.[119]

The nerves at the top of the spinal cord control unconscious tasks, such as breathing. If the top of the spinal cord is[142] damaged, these unconscious tasks can stop, and the person can die.[153]

KEY NOTES

The Super-Highway
What does the spinal cord do?

_____

_____

The Human Nervous System

What Does the Nervous System Do?

1. Which of the following BEST tells what the human nervous system does?

  a. It helps you calm down if you're nervous.
  b. It manages your body's other systems.
  c. It helps you control your spinal cord.
  d. It works with your unconscious responses.

2. Which of the following are parts of the human nervous system?

  a. the brain, the eyes, and the nose
  b. the spinal cord, the nerves, and the heart
  c. the brain, the spinal cord, and the nerves
  d. the arms, the legs, and the hands

3. What is the difference between a conscious response and an unconscious response?

_____

_____

_____

The Control Center

1. What do the nerves do?

  a. protect the spinal cord
  b. keep the brain safe
  c. receive and carry information to the brain
  d. tell the brain how to control the cerebrum

2. What are the three main parts of the brain?

_____

_____

_____

3. What does the cerebellum do?

_____

_____

_____

Sending Messages

1. Sensory neurons send information _____

    a. from the brain to the senses.
    b. from the brain to the muscles.
    c. from the senses to the brain.
    d. from the hands to the legs.

2. Motor neurons send information _____

    a. from the legs to the hands.
    b. from the heart to the brain.
    c. from the brain to the senses.
    d. from the brain to the muscles.

3. How do neurons send information through the body?

_____

_____

_____

The Super-Highway

1. What is the spinal cord made of?

    a. the backbones
    b. the brain and muscles
    c. bundles of nerves
    d. all of the nerves in the body

2. How is the nervous system like a super-highway?

_____

_____

_____

3. What can happen if a person's spinal cord is damaged?

_____

_____

_____

nervous	conscious	unconscious	cerebrum	cerebellum
brainstem	sensory	neuron	paralyzed	

1. Choose the word from the word box above that best matches each definition. Write the word on the line below.

A. _____ nerve cells that send messages to and from the brain

B. _____ relating to the nerves in the body

C. _____ the part of the brain that controls thought and reasoning

D. _____ aware of things that are happening around you

E. _____ relating to the senses, including touch and sight

F. _____ the part of the brain that controls muscle movement and balance

G. _____ a response that does not involve thinking

H. _____ a bundle of nerves at the base of the brain

I. _____ not able to move

2. Fill in the blanks in the sentences below. Choose the word from the word box that completes each sentence.

A. _____ carry messages along the nerves in the body.

B. Memories are stored in the _____.

C. _____ neurons tell your brain what goes on around you.

D. The _____ helps you walk, sit, and move your hands.

E. The _____ system controls everything the body does.

F. Rob wasn't _____ that the teacher had called on him because he was daydreaming.

G. Jim was _____ when his spinal cord was damaged in an accident.

H. Your _____ controls such basic jobs in the body as breathing and sleeping.

I. Pulling your hand away from a hot pan is an _____ response.

The Human Nervous System

A. nervous system _____

B. brain _____

C. spinal cord _____

D. nerves _____

E. cerebellum _____

F. cerebrum _____

G. brainstem _____

H. sensory neurons _____

I. motor neurons _____

2. Describe a conscious response a person might have.

_____

_____

_____

_____

3. Describe an unconscious response a person might have.

_____

_____

_____

_____

4. Describe three things your nervous system does every day.

_____

_____

_____

_____

Environmental Disasters

Clearing of a forest can lead to an environmental disaster.

Fast Facts

- In 1989, an oil tanker leaked about 11,000,000 gallons of oil into the ocean off Alaska.

- It has been estimated that this oil spill killed 250,000 seabirds and 2,800 sea otters.

- In 2004, a huge wave killed more than 200,000 people in Asia.

What Causes Environmental Disasters?

When an environmental disaster occurs, large numbers of plants and animals, and even Earth itself, are damaged.[21] Sometimes one event, like a ship spilling oil into the ocean, causes the damage. At other times, the damage can be caused by activities that happen over many years.[50]

Currently, Haiti is suffering from environmental damage caused by years of forest clearing. In 1950, about 2 of every[69] 5 square miles of Haiti were covered with forest. Since that time, people have cut down millions of trees to make space for[92] farmland and to get firewood to burn. Today, only about 1 of every 100 square miles of Haiti is covered with forest.[114]

Clearing so much forest has led to many environmental problems. With few trees to hold the soil in place, heavy rains[135] create floods that kill people and wash away the topsoil that is needed to grow food.[151]

KEY NOTES

What Causes Environmental Disasters?
What can cause an environmental disaster?

_____

_____

Environmental Disasters

Smog can make people sick.

Fast Facts

- In 1952–1953, about 12,000 people died from deadly smog in London.

- As a result of this disaster, the British government passed the Clean Air Act.

- In 1991, a volcano in Asia threw tons of dust and gas into the air, creating an environmental disaster.

Killer Smog

On Tuesday, October 26, 1948, heavy fog settled into a narrow river valley in Pennsylvania. For years, people in the[22] valley had lived with smoke from a factory that smelted, or separated, metal from ore. Usually, the smoke was carried away[43] into the air. On this day, though, the fog held the smoke near the ground. Because no fresh air could get in to blow the smoke away, the fog and smoke formed a thick smog.[78]

The smog stayed in the Pennsylvania valley for almost a week. During this time, although many people had trouble breathing, the smelting factory kept producing smoke.[104]

Finally, on Sunday, the smelting factory was shut down, and rain arrived and began to break up the smog. By that time,[126] however, 7,000 people had become sick and 20 people had died. This environmental disaster led to the first state and federal laws that control the quality of air.[154]

KEY NOTES

Killer Smog

What is smog?

_____

_____

Environmental Disasters

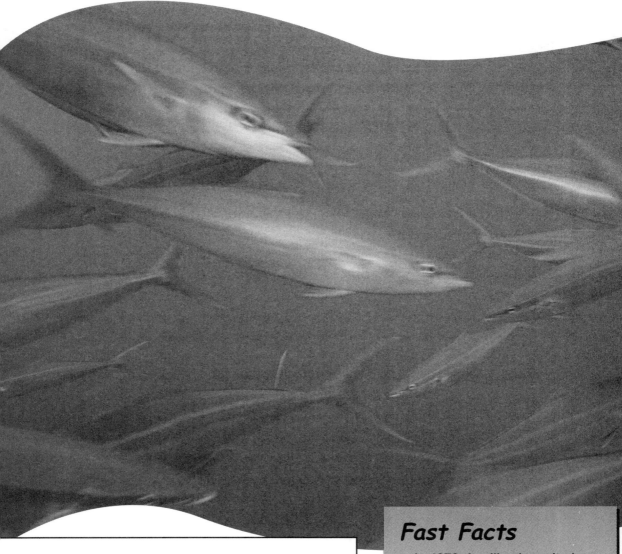

Mercury affects fish, animals, and people.

Fast Facts

- In 1978, families in a city in New York lived on land that contained deadly chemicals.

- In 1984, a factory in India released a gas into the air, killing thousands of people.

- In 2000, a chemical spill at a gold mine in Europe released deadly substances into three rivers.

Deadly Substances

In the 1940s, people living in a seaside town in Japan noticed that cats and other animals were acting strangely.[22] Some cats seemed to dance into the sea, where they drowned. By the 1950s, some people in the town were also acting[44] strangely. By 1956, many of the people were very ill and others had died. Finally, it was found that a local company had been[68] spilling mercury compounds into the bay near the town for more than 20 years.[82]

The people and the animals of the town had been eating fish from the bay for many years. Scientists found that the fish[105] had deposits of mercury compounds in their bodies. As people and animals ate the fish, deposits of mercury compounds[124] built up inside them and made them sick. This environmental disaster showed that deadly substances can get into the food chain and can harm many species.[150]

KEY NOTES

Deadly Substances

How did people know something was wrong in the Japanese town?

_____

_____

Environmental Disasters

The Three Mile Island nuclear reactors are near a river.

Fast Facts

- Soon after the Chernobyl accident, 31 people were reported killed.

- Government figures now report that thousands of people have died since the accident.

- Radioactive material released at Chernobyl continues to affect people today.

Nuclear Accidents

Nuclear power plants can provide large amounts of cheap energy. However, accidents at nuclear power plants can be costly[21] to people, animals, and the environment. A nuclear explosion throws radiation into the air that can be very harmful to all[42] living things. Radiation in the soil affects plants for years. Radioactive particles in the air or in food can cause serious health problems for people and animals.[69]

In 1986, the world's biggest nuclear accident happened near Chernobyl, a small city in eastern Europe. Several large[87] explosions at a nuclear power plant were followed by fires. Almost 9 tons of radioactive material escaped into the air and[108] seeped into the soil. More than 100,000 people were moved from Chernobyl to escape the danger. For several years afterward,[128] hundreds of thousands of workers tried to clean up the radioactive material. Even so, many people became ill from high levels of radiation.[151]

KEY NOTES

Nuclear Accidents
What caused the environmental disaster in Chernobyl?

_____

_____

Environmental Disasters

What Causes Environmental Disasters?

1. Which of the following BEST describes an environmental disaster?

    a. damage to farmlands and forests
    b. living things that damage one another
    c. forest clearings that damage a species
    d. damage to large numbers of plants and animals

2. How long does it take for an environmental disaster to occur?

_____

_____

_____

3. How did human activity in Haiti cause environmental damage there?

_____

_____

_____

Killer Smog

1. The killer smog in Pennsylvania came from _____

    a. a power plant in another state.
    b. a factory in the valley.
    c. rain that fell for weeks.
    d. poisoned water in the river.

2. How did the factory smoke become an environmental disaster?

_____

_____

_____

3. How did people try to keep a smog disaster from happening again?

_____

_____

_____

Deadly Substances

1. What was an early sign that something was wrong in the Japanese town?

    a. There were fewer fish in the bay.
    b. A local factory fired some workers.
    c. Animals and people were acting strangely.
    d. People started to eat fish from the bay.

2. What caused the environmental disaster in Japan?

    a. A factory was dumping mercury compounds into the bay.
    b. Animals and people were acting strangely.
    c. People were eating mercury compounds at the factory.
    d. Environmental laws in Japan were too strict.

3. How did the mercury compounds get into people's bodies?

_____

_____

_____

Nuclear Accidents

1. What is one way nuclear power plants are helpful?

    a. They can solve environmental problems.

    b. They can provide cheap energy.

    c. They can prevent environmental disasters.

    d. They can keep radiation from harming the environment.

2. What is one way nuclear power plants can be harmful?

_____

_____

_____

3. How do you know that the accident at Chernobyl was very serious?

_____

_____

_____

environmental	disaster	Haiti	Pennsylvania
compounds	nuclear	radiation	Chernobyl

1. Choose the word from the word box above that best matches each definition. Write the word on the line below.

A. _____ the act of giving off energy that moves in all directions

B. _____ a town in eastern Europe where a serious nuclear accident happened

C. _____ a state in the eastern United States

D. _____ relating to power that comes from the center of atoms

E. _____ an island country in North America

F. _____ things made by combining two or more separate things

G. _____ something that happens quickly and causes a lot of damage

H. _____ relating to things that happen in nature

2. Fill in the blanks in the sentences below. Choose the word from the word box that completes each sentence.

A. _____ is a state that is near New York and New Jersey.

B. Mercury _____ released into the bay in Japan made animals and people sick.

C. The nuclear power plant released _____ into the air.

D. After the nuclear accident at _____, thousands of people had to leave the area.

E. Cutting huge numbers of trees in _____ caused floods that washed away topsoil.

F. _____ power can make lots of electrical power, but it can cause problems, too.

G. The oil spill created a _____ that killed many fish.

H. New _____ laws have been passed to keep Earth safer.

Environmental Disasters

1. Use the chart to help you remember what you read. In the left column, describe the type of environmental disaster in each location. In the right column, describe the cause of each environmental disaster.

Type of Environmental Disaster	Cause
A. Haiti	_____ _____ _____ _____
B. Pennsylvania	_____ _____ _____ _____
C. Japan	_____ _____ _____ _____
D. Chernobyl	_____ _____ _____ _____

2. Describe how two kinds of environmental disasters can harm people, animals, and plants.

_____

_____

_____

_____

3. Why do you think people do things that can cause environmental disasters?

_____

_____

_____

_____

4. Describe two ways environmental disasters could be prevented.

_____

_____

_____

_____

Computers

Computers make writing easier.

Fast Facts

- Most computers process words, pictures, and sounds by translating them into electrical charges.

- The first electronic digital computer was completed in 1942.

- One of the first electronic computers was so big that it weighed 30 tons.

What Is a Computer?

A computer is a machine that can be programmed to do a range of tasks. Computers organize, process, store, and display[25] information. However, computers are changing so quickly that this description may not be complete for very long.[42]

Computers perform their tasks at lightning speed. They are programmed to carry out huge numbers of calculations in[60] seconds. In addition to calculations, they can be used to create, edit, and store books, music, and movies.[78]

Before computers were invented, people wrote everything by hand or with typewriters. Writing in this way did not allow[97] people to change their work easily. With a computer, though, writers can change a few words or a whole paragraph in only a few seconds.[122]

Computers can also communicate with other computers over short or long distances. This feature makes it possible for people[141] to send words, music, and pictures around the world in seconds.[152]

KEY NOTES

What Is a Computer?
What tasks are done by computers?

_____

_____

Computers

The network server is one type of computer hardware.

Fast Facts

- Modern processors no bigger than a fingernail are faster and can do more than the first electronic computer.

- Supercomputers can have hundreds of processors operating together.

- Personal computers were introduced in 1975.

Computer Hardware

Most computers contain several components, or pieces. They have a processor and memory, input, and output devices.[19] They also have wiring that connects these components. These computer parts are called hardware.[33]

The processor makes calculations and logical decisions. Memory devices store data and the instructions for what the[50] processor should do with the data. Input devices, like a mouse and keyboard, allow users to tell the computer what to do.[72] Output devices, like a screen and a printer, show users what the computer has done.[87]

Most computers have two kinds of memory devices. Information that's needed often and quickly is stored on memory[105] chips. These chips have no moving parts and store small amounts of data. Larger amounts of information are usually[124] stored on a hard drive, a compact disc (CD), or a digital video disc (DVD). Compact discs, digital video discs, and hard drives are also known as computer hardware.[153]

KEY NOTES

Computer Hardware
What is computer hardware?

_____

_____

Computers

Programmers write software for computer games.

Fast Facts

- Digital computers use only the numbers 1 and 0 to store information.

- In computer language, a single 0 or 1 is called a bit, which stands for "binary digit."

- The first video game was created in 1958. It was called Tennis for Two.

Computer Software

Computer hardware is useless without software. Software controls what happens inside a computer. Several computer[17] languages have been developed for writing software. For a computer to do a task, the software for that task must be written[39] in the same language as the software that runs the computer. When computers and software use the same language, they are compatible, or able to be used together.[67]

There are two types of computer software. System software manages the computer's hardware. It also does other tasks,[85] such as moving data into memory and showing information on the screen. System software acts like an umbrella, allowing applications to operate underneath it.[109]

Application software does specific tasks, such as processing words and playing music and movies. Application software[125] usually works under the umbrella of the system software. No matter what kind of software is used, though, it must be compatible with the computer that runs it.[153]

KEY NOTES

Computer Software
What does computer software do?

_____

_____

Computers

A forensics expert looks at someone else's hard drive as part of her job.

Fast Facts

- In 2004, about 518,000 technical support workers in the United States had an average salary of $40,000.

- In 2004, about 455,000 programmers in the U.S. had an average salary of $63,900.

- In 2004, about 525,000 information processing workers in the U.S. had an average salary of $28,000.

Computer Jobs

The wide use of computers has led to many computer-related jobs. Computer hardware engineers design new computers.[20] These engineers work every day on ways to make computers faster and more dependable. People who write computer software[39] are called programmers. Programmers create and test the software that's used by computers. When people have trouble[56] using computers, they call technical support workers. Technical support workers fix the machines and show people how to use their computers properly.[78]

Some companies that have many computers link them to form a network. People called network administrators or systems[96] administrators manage these networks. They make sure that the network runs properly, that the computers can send and receive[115] information, and that the people can get and use the information they need.[128]

Two other computer-related jobs are data entry and information processing. People who do this work enter information into computers so others can use it.[153]

KEY NOTES

Computer Jobs
What are three types of computer-related jobs?

_____

_____

Computers

What Is a Computer?

1. The main idea of "What Is a Computer?" is that _____

    a. computers are used by many people today.
    b. computers help us do many things.
    c. computers are difficult to understand.
    d. computers will be more useful in the future.

2. What can computers be programmed to do?

    a. write people's work
    b. perform calculations quickly
    c. listen to music sent over long distances
    d. all of the above

3. Describe two ways computers have changed the way people do things.

_____

_____

_____

Computer Hardware

1. Another good name for "Computer Hardware" is _____

    a. "How to Use a Computer."
    b. "Inventing Computers."
    c. "The Parts of a Computer."
    d. "Changes in Computers."

2. What do computer input and output devices do?

_____

_____

_____

3. In what two ways is information stored on a computer?

_____

_____

_____

Computer Software

1. What is software?

    a. instructions that control what happens in a computer
    b. the parts of a computer that work together
    c. the languages that computer programmers use
    d. how a computer system does its tasks

2. What is a program?

    a. the system that runs a computer's software
    b. a set of instructions for a task
    c. application software that works as an umbrella
    d. a language for writing software

3. What is the difference between system software and application software?

_____

_____

_____

Computer Jobs

1. What are computer networks?

    a. a group of computers that are in the same room
    b. a way to connect computers that use the same language
    c. a group of computers that are linked together
    d. all of the above

2. What do technical support workers do?

_____

_____

_____

3. Compare two of the computer-related jobs discussed in this passage.

_____

_____

_____

programmed	components	processor	memory
compatible	application	engineers	technical

1. Choose the word from the word box above that best matches each definition. Write the word on the line below.

A. _____ relating to subjects that need special knowledge or training

B. _____ given a set of instructions to do something

C. _____ the part of a computer that makes decisions about how to complete tasks

D. _____ relating to a computer program that does a specific task

E. _____ people who use scientific knowledge to design and build things

F. _____ parts of something

G. _____ the part of a computer that stores information

H. _____ designed to work together easily

2. Fill in the blanks in the sentences below. Choose the word from the word box that completes each sentence.

A. The _____ of toast are bread and butter.

B. Kate can't run her new software because it's not _____ with her computer.

C. Fixing computers is a _____ job that requires a lot of training and skill.

D. Paul _____ his computer so that no one could use it without his password.

E. A computer's _____ is like a human brain because both save information.

F. Computer _____ created the flat-screen monitors.

G. Rico's new _____ is faster and runs more programs than his old one did.

H. Word-processing programs are one kind of _____ software.

131

Computers

1. Use the chart to help you remember what you read. Draw a line from each term on the left to its definition on the right.

Term

A. computer processor

B. mouse and keyboard

C. screen and printer

D. memory chip

E. system software

F. application software

G. hardware engineers

H. programmers

I. system administrators

J. data entry

Definition

does specific tasks, such as processing words and playing music and movies

people who write computer software

people who manage computer networks

putting information into computers

people who design new computers

stores information that's needed often and quickly

show people what the computer has done

hardware that makes calculations and logical decisions

manages the computer's hardware

help people to tell the computer what to do

2. How have computers made people's everyday life easier?

_____

_____

_____

_____

3. How were early computers different from the computers sold today?

_____

_____

_____

_____

4. How do you think computers of the future will be different from today's computers?

_____

_____

_____

_____

Murals

This mural in Italy was painted on plaster in about 500 B.C.

Fast Facts

- The world's largest mural is 2 miles long and 58 feet tall.

- In California, there is a mural made of 100,000 pennies.

- The world's largest hotel mural is in China. It is 16 stories high.

What Are Murals?

A mural is a picture created for a wall. Murals can be painted or drawn on a building's interior or exterior walls. Most[26] murals are what is called public art. This means they are meant to be seen by many people.[44]

Murals are one of the oldest forms of art. Thousands of years ago, people drew pictures of animals on the walls of[66] caves. Murals were painted by the ancient Egyptians, Greeks, and Romans. Murals were very popular in Europe, especially[84] Italy, from the 1300s to the 1500s. During the 1920s, painters in Mexico used murals to show Mexican history. In the 1930s and[107] early 1940s, the U.S. government hired artists to create murals for public buildings.[120]

Today, exterior murals are common in many places. Interior murals are common inside older buildings. Murals are often[138] painted by people in a community working together to create a work of art. They can help give people pride in their history, city, or neighborhood.[164]

KEY NOTES

What Are Murals?
How have murals changed over time?

_____

_____

Murals

Diego Rivera painted many murals.

Fast Facts

- Diego Rivera was born in 1886 and died in 1957.

- Rivera's first mural had figures that were more than 12 feet tall.

- Rivera painted 124 pictures on the courtyard walls of a government building in Mexico.

Diego Rivera

One artist who made murals popular in Mexico was Diego Rivera. Rivera started drawing before he was two years[21] old. When he was 10, he knew he wanted to be an artist. Rivera went to art school in Mexico and later studied art in Europe.[47]

In Italy, Rivera saw murals on church walls. He liked the idea that everyone could see art around them, and he wanted to make art available to the people of Mexico.[78]

When Rivera returned to Mexico, he painted murals on the walls of government buildings. He drew large people and used[98] bright colors. His murals portrayed Mexican life and history, and they made Rivera famous. The historical murals portrayed[116] events from Mexico's past. Mexican people could view the historical murals and be proud of their past and their art.[136]

Today, some of Rivera's best-known murals can be seen in the National Palace in Mexico City. His murals are also in public places in the United States.[164]

KEY NOTES

Diego Rivera
Who was Diego Rivera?

_____

_____

Murals

A mural in San Francisco shows a cooking scene.

Fast Facts

- Pictures in a San Francisco tower were created by 26 artists and 19 assistants.

- The Diego Rivera mural at a college theater in San Francisco measures 22 feet by 74 feet.

- One San Francisco mural is four stories high.

Murals in San Francisco

San Francisco is known for its hills. It is also known for its murals. There are more than 600 murals on the interior and[28] exterior walls of San Francisco's landmarks and other buildings. Four of these murals were painted by Diego Rivera.[46]

One of Rivera's murals, which is at an art school, shows the building of a city. Another Rivera mural is at a theater in[70] a college. This mural shows the mixing of North and South American cultural ideas.[84]

Among San Francisco's landmarks is a tower. Inside this tower are murals that show farming, industry, education, and[102] life in California. The artists who painted these pictures were hired by the U.S. government.[117]

San Francisco also has two alleys that have murals on both sides. One of these alleys has walking tours in which people[139] learn about the murals. In the other alley, there's a party every year to show off new murals that are added.[160]

KEY NOTES
Murals in San Francisco
What kinds of murals can be seen in San Francisco?
_____
_____

Murals

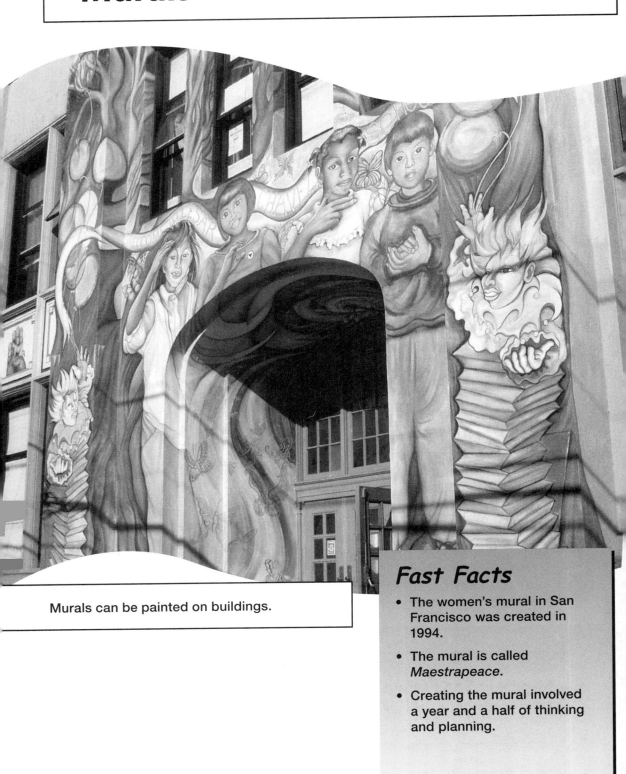

Murals can be painted on buildings.

Fast Facts

- The women's mural in San Francisco was created in 1994.
- The mural is called *Maestrapeace*.
- Creating the mural involved a year and a half of thinking and planning.

A Mural for Women

One mural in San Francisco was designed to honor women. It stretches across two walls of a four-story women's center.[25] This mural is a tribute to women and depicts their many contributions to society all over the world.[43]

The artwork includes many pictures of women. Some of the women are famous, and some are unknown. The mural is[63] a tribute to women's successes in art and science, and to their contributions to society throughout history. The mural depicts[83] girls and women of all ages. It also has many images of nature and food. More than 100 women worked to create it.[106]

The seven artists who were the main creative force behind the mural are also art teachers. They wanted this artwork to[127] encourage people to think about how to achieve justice, peace, and creativity through art. Two of the artists have called[147] the mural "a commitment to a healthier future for all of our children."[160]

KEY NOTES

A Mural for Women
Why was the women's mural painted?

_____

_____

Murals

What Are Murals?

1. What is a mural?

    a. a picture created for a wall
    b. a person who poses for a picture
    c. a picture about history
    d. a person who creates art

2. How long have people been creating murals?

    a. since people had modern tools
    b. since there were buildings
    c. since people lived in caves
    d. since the 1300s

3. Why do people paint murals today?

_____

_____

_____

Diego Rivera

1. What did Diego Rivera do?

    a. He painted murals for churches in Italy.
    b. He painted murals in Mexico.
    c. He painted murals for the U.S. government.
    d. He painted murals for museums.

2. What did Rivera portray in his murals?

_____

_____

_____

3. How did the murals Rivera saw in Italy change the way he thought about art?

_____

_____

_____

Murals in San Francisco

1. Where are the murals in San Francisco?

    a. in U.S. government buildings
    b. on the buildings on the sides of the hills
    c. on the exterior walls of buildings
    d. in landmarks, buildings, and alleys

2. From this passage, you could conclude that _____

    a. most murals in San Francisco were painted by Diego Rivera.
    b. it would not take long to find a mural in San Francisco.
    c. San Francisco has a lot of buildings.
    d. the artists of San Francisco create many kinds of art.

3. Based on this passage, what do you think the people of San Francisco think about art?

_____

_____

_____

A Mural for Women

1. The mural described in the passage shows _____

    a. women's contributions to society.
    b. the women of San Francisco.
    c. women who teach art.
    d. women's contributions to buildings.

2. What images are included in this mural?

_____

_____

_____

3. Why do you think the mural includes pictures of women who are unknown as well as women who are famous?

_____

_____

_____

mural	exterior	interior	portrayed	historical
landmarks	tribute	depicts	contributions	

1. Choose the word from the word box above that best matches each definition. Write the word on the line below.

A. _____ things that are important because of their history or beauty

B. _____ a picture created for a wall

C. _____ showed something in a certain way

D. _____ being on the outside of something

E. _____ something that honors something or someone

F. _____ being on the inside of something

G. _____ involving things that happened in the past

H. _____ shown in a painting or in words

I. _____ things that are given to others

2. Fill in the blanks in the sentences below. Choose the word from the word box that completes each sentence.

A. Her painting was done to _____ things women have invented.

B. The art was a _____ to the brave people of the town.

C. The _____ walls of buildings are good places for murals.

D. The play _____ a man's search for his brother.

E. The mural showed the _____ of all cultures to our town's history.

F. A huge _____ covered the entire wall.

G. One reason to visit a city is to see its famous _____.

H. Art that deals with the past is _____.

I. I wanted the _____ walls of our house to be painted in bright colors.

Murals

1. Use the idea web to help you remember what you read. In each box, write the main idea of that passage.

What Are Murals?

_____

_____

_____

_____

Diego Rivera

_____

_____

_____

_____

Murals

Murals in San Francisco

_____

_____

_____

A Mural for Women

_____

_____

_____

2. How are murals different from other kinds of art?

_____

_____

_____

_____

3. Why do you think some murals have a great effect on people?

_____

_____

_____

_____

4. If you planned a mural for your school or your neighborhood, what would you show?

_____

_____

_____

_____

Amazing Architecture

A house designed by Frank Lloyd Wright has its own waterfall.

Fast Facts

- Architecture is one of the oldest arts.

- The first important architecture appeared in the Middle East more than 5,000 years ago.

- In 2004, about 129,000 people worked as architects in the United States.

What Is Architecture?

Every building was designed by someone. People who design buildings and other structures are called architects.[19] Architects create office buildings, houses, schools, factories, hospitals, theaters, and other structures. The art and science of designing buildings is called architecture.[41]

Architects think about a building carefully before construction begins. They envision how the building will[56] look. Appearance is important because people like to live in attractive places. Architects also think about how the building[75] will be used. An office must be a place where people can work comfortably. A school should be designed so that students can[98] easily find their classrooms. In addition, architects envision how people will take care of the structure. A building should last a long time without needing expensive repairs.[125]

In the United States, there are many kinds of architecture, from American Indian buildings that are hundreds of years old[145] to modern homes and sports stadiums. These are just three examples of the architecture in our world.[162]

KEY NOTES

What Is Architecture?
What do architects do?

_____

_____

Amazing Architecture

Ladders connected rooms in pueblos.

Fast Facts

- In Colorado, there are Pueblo Indian dwellings that were built in the 1200s.

- One pueblo in New Mexico may have 800 rooms.

- The straw and mud bricks used to build some pueblos are called adobe.

Pueblo Dwellings

Hundreds of years ago, several groups of American Indians created a new style of architecture with buildings that were[21] several stories high. Spanish people who came to the American Southwest called these people the *Pueblo*, a Spanish word that[41] means "town." Today, this word refers to both American Indians and their dwellings. The people of the Pueblo Indians are from[62] different American Indian groups, but all of them built similar dwellings.[73]

Pueblo dwellings had many rooms. Some were made of earth mixed with straw and water. This mixture was often made[93] into bricks that were dried in the sun. Logs helped support the roof, which was made by laying smaller pieces of wood side by[117] side on the logs and covering them with dirt. In the pueblos, people used ladders to get from one level to another. If a pueblo[142] was attacked, people pulled the ladders up. Today, Pueblo dwellings can be seen in Colorado and New Mexico.[160]

KEY NOTES

Pueblo Dwellings
What kind of dwellings did Pueblo Indians build?

_____

_____

Amazing Architecture

Dome houses are built on circular frames.

Fast Facts

- A-frame houses are good for snowy areas because snow does not pile up on the roof.

- The building that became the first dome house was introduced in 1948.

- The person who created the dome house later built a dome that was 20 stories high.

Modern Homes

When architects design homes, they often consult with the people who will live in them. They consult so they know what[23] kind of house the people want. Architects also create unusual homes they think people might like. Two of these designs— A-frames and domes—have become popular.[49]

A-frame houses are shaped like a big A. They are usually erected in the country and are often used as vacation homes.[71] A-frames have a lot of room at the bottom, which might be one big open space. The top of the house has less room because the house comes to a point.[102]

Another unusual home design is the dome. A modern dome house is built on a circular frame divided into many small[123] sections. The frame is covered, and the finished house looks like half of a soccer ball. Dome houses are easy to build, do not[147] require much space, and are not expensive. They are also most commonly erected in the country.[163]

KEY NOTES

Modern Homes
What kinds of unusual modern homes have architects designed?

_____

_____

Amazing Architecture

Stadiums with retractable roofs are used for sports and events.

Fast Facts

- The SkyDome cost $500 million to build.

- When the roof of the SkyDome is closed, a 31-story building can fit inside the stadium.

- The roof of the SkyDome weighs 11,000 tons.

Sports Stadiums

Architects also design new stadiums, or places where sports and other big events take place. Most stadiums are either outdoor or[23] indoor stadiums. However, in 1989 a new kind of stadium, the SkyDome, opened in Canada.[38]

The SkyDome is both an outdoor and an indoor stadium because it has a retractable roof. When the roof is open, it's an[61] outdoor stadium. When the roof is closed, it's an indoor stadium. The SkyDome was also new in another way—inside the stadium[83] is a hotel with 348 rooms. In 2005, the SkyDome was renamed the Rogers Centre.[98]

Today, stadiums with retractable roofs are common. They can be used all year, in any weather. Many are used for more than one sport.[122]

Retractable roofs for huge stadiums were a challenge for architects, because stadium roofs weigh many tons and have[140] no poles to support them. Each time architects meet such a challenge, it's a reminder of how amazing architecture can be.[161]

KEY NOTES

Sports Stadiums
How are new sports stadiums different from older stadiums?

_____

_____

Amazing Architecture

What Is Architecture?

1. Architecture is _____

    a. the study of American Indian buildings.
    b. the art and science of designing buildings.
    c. the study of home construction.
    d. the art and science of designing paintings.

2. In this passage, *envision* means _____

    a. a kind of architecture.
    b. seeing a movie about something.
    c. having a picture in the mind.
    d. wondering how something will look.

3. What three things do architects think about before building construction begins?

_____

_____

_____

Pueblo Dwellings

1. The word *pueblo* refers to _____

    a. groups of American Indians and their crops.
    b. the southwestern part of the United States.
    c. a style of architecture used by Spanish people.
    d. groups of American Indians and their architecture.

2. Describe how Pueblo Indian dwellings were made.

_____

_____

_____

3. How did people living in pueblos keep themselves safe?

_____

_____

_____

Modern Homes

1. An A-frame house _____

    a. has more room at the bottom than at the top.

    b. is shaped like a dome.

    c. is very popular in cities.

    d. has more room at the top than at the bottom.

2. Dome houses are _____

    a. built on a circular frame.

    b. pointed at the top.

    c. shaped like a football.

    d. designed to be built in cities.

3. Why might people want to consult with the architect who is designing their home?

_____

_____

_____

Sports Stadiums

1. What was different about the SkyDome?

    a. It had a lot of seats.
    b. It was built in Canada.
    c. It had a retractable roof.
    d. It had seats arranged in a circle.

2. Why is a retractable roof a good idea for a stadium?

_____

_____

_____

3. Why is creating a retractable roof for a stadium a challenge?

_____

_____

_____

| architecture | envision | pueblo | dwellings |
| consult | erected | stadium | retractable |

1. Choose the word from the word box above that best matches each definition. Write the word on the line below.

A. _____ to get a picture in the mind or form an idea about something

B. _____ a building made by American Indians in the Southwest

C. _____ built

D. _____ a large structure with many seats used for sports events

E. _____ able to be pulled back

F. _____ to talk about together

G. _____ the art and science of designing buildings

H. _____ places where people live

2. Fill in the blanks in the sentences below. Choose the word from the word box that completes each sentence.

A. The stadium's roof was _____, so it could be opened and closed.

B. Architects often discuss their plans when designing _____.

C. Paul wanted to design homes, so he studied _____.

D. When Laura was in the Southwest, she visited an American Indian _____.

E. The architect kept getting new ideas as the building he designed was being _____.

F. As we listened to Robert describe the museum, it was easy to _____ it.

G. Next week, we're meeting with an architect to _____ with her about how our new office should look.

H. The _____ was filled with people eager to see the athletes compete.

Amazing Architecture

1. Use the chart to help you remember what you read. On each line, write a brief description for each word or phrase in the left column.

A. retractable roof _____

_____

_____

B. architecture _____

_____

_____

C. sports stadium _____

_____

_____

D. pueblo _____

_____

_____

E. dome house _____

_____

_____

F. architect _____

_____

_____

G. A-frame house _____

_____

_____

2. Compare two kinds of architecture you read about in this topic.

_____

_____

_____

_____

3. How might designing a house be different from designing a school?

_____

_____

_____

_____

4. Think about the architecture in your school or another building in your town. What do you think the architect thought about when it was being designed?

_____

_____

_____

_____

Designing for All

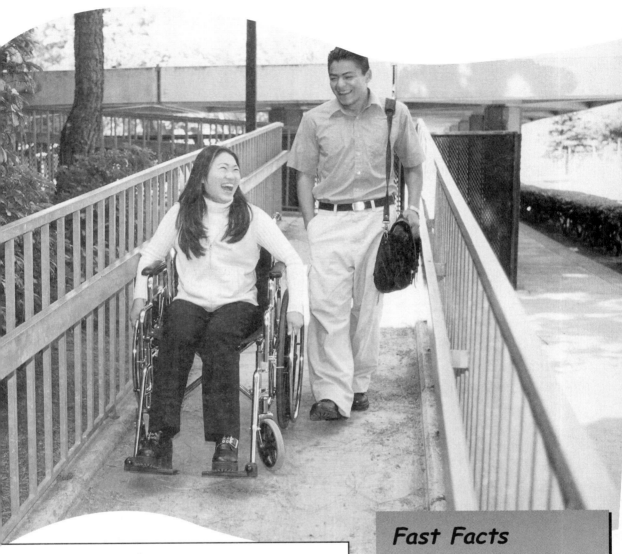

A ramp is one feature of universal design.

Fast Facts

- In 2003, about 39 million people in the United States five years and older had a disability.

- Of this number, more than 3 million were 5-17 years old.

- Since 1968, the U.S. government has passed at least six laws to help people with disabilities.

What Is Universal Design?

The products we use and places like buildings and playgrounds aren't just built; they are designed. To design something is to think about it and create it according to a plan.[35]

Some people might not pay attention to how things are designed. However, some people have physical disabilities.[52] Perhaps they're sick, have been in an accident, or have been hurt in war. For people with disabilities, things like stairs, or[74] even one step, can be an obstruction. However, if products and places are designed carefully, life becomes easier for us all. That's where universal design comes in.[101]

Universal design is the creation of products and environments that can easily be used by everyone. An example[119] of universal design is a ramp at the entrance to a building. The ramp can be used by people who have no problem with[143] stairs and by people for whom steps might be an obstruction. That's just one way universal design helps everyone.[162]

KEY NOTES

What Is Universal Design?
Why are buildings and playgrounds designed?

_____

_____

Designing for All

Older homes can use universal design, too.

Fast Facts

- To be accessible to people in wheelchairs, doorways should be at least 32 inches wide.

- A ramp leading to a doorway should be at least 36 inches wide.

- Different colors in a room help people who cannot see well.

At Home

When we think about making places accessible to people with disabilities, we often think of places like office buildings,[21] restaurants, and hotels. However, homes can also be made accessible.[31]

Some people believe that homes should be built so that they're accessible to everyone. One way to build an accessible[51] house is to have no steps at the main entrance. Another way is to build wide doorways that allow people who use wheelchairs to easily get into every room.[80]

Houses that have already been built can easily be made accessible, too. One way to make a house accessible is to install[102] special faucets and to put switches in accessible places. These changes can help people who don't have much strength or who[123] can't reach far to turn on lights. Another way to increase accessibility is to install grab bars in places like bathrooms.[144] People can hold grab bars while they get in and out of a bathtub or shower.[160]

KEY NOTES

At Home
How can universal design be used in homes?

_____

_____

Designing for All

Universal design can be used everywhere, including summer camps.

Fast Facts

- Braille was named after Louis Braille, who taught blind students in France.

- Braille, who was blind, developed the writing system when he was 15 years old.

- According to the U.S. government, about 28 million Americans have difficulty hearing.

In School and at Work

Schools and work settings should be accessible to everyone so that all people, including those with disabilities, can attend school[25] or work at almost any job. In fact, a law called the Americans with Disabilities Act of 1990 says that people with disabilities have the same rights to employment as everyone else.[57]

Schools can do several things to help students with disabilities. In addition to ramps for students in wheelchairs,[75] schools can install lifts that raise and lower wheelchairs. For students who have trouble seeing, schools can get books with large print or books in Braille.[101]

Offices can do similar things. They can provide reading material in Braille. They can provide computers that present[119] information in both audio and visual forms. For workers who have hearing disabilities, offices can provide telephones with audio[138] controls that can make sounds louder. In addition, offices can provide telephone systems for deaf people that use flashing lights instead of ring tones.[162]

KEY NOTES

In School and at Work
How can design help people with disabilities in school and at work?

_____

_____

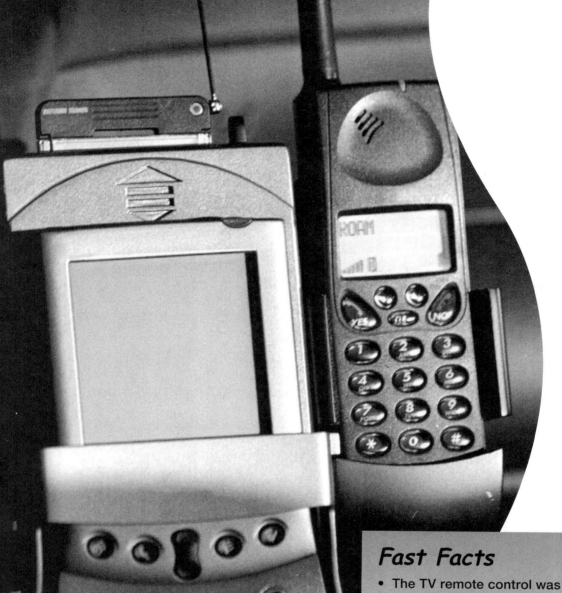

Voice-activated controls help people and machines do tasks.

Fast Facts

- The TV remote control was developed in 1950. It was called Lazy Bones.

- The first TV remote controls were connected to the television with a wire.

- In 1984, a voice-activated wheelchair was used for the first time.

Technology Helps

Modern technology is making universal design easier to achieve and more common. Voice-activated phones help people[19] who can't reach a telephone. This includes people who can't move because of a disability and doctors who can't move because they[41] are performing an operation. One common example of universal design that helps everyone is TV and radio remote controls.[60]

Modern technology is also creating new things that help people with disabilities. Voice-activated lights let people turn[78] lights on and off from across a room. Voice-activated computers let people operate computers by talking to them. Special warning[99] systems summon help for people who can't move because they're hurt.[110]

In addition, some "smart homes" have many machines that[119] can be operated by remote control. Remote controls can operate a home's temperature, lights, and entertainment equipment. It[137] can also summon help if people are sick or hurt. Technology like this helps us all, and that's what universal design is all about.[161]

KEY NOTES

Technology Helps

How can technology help people with and without disabilities?

_____

_____

Designing for All

What Is Universal Design?

1. Universal design is _____

    a. the creation of products and environments that can easily be used by wheelchairs.
    b. the study of how the universe was created.
    c. the study of how to design houses and offices.
    d. the creation of products and environments that can easily be used by everyone.

2. One example of universal design is _____

    a. a short set of stairs.
    b. an elevator.
    c. a door that opens to the outside.
    d. an indoor parking garage.

3. How is a ramp placed at the entrance to a building an example of universal design?

    _____

    _____

    _____

At Home

1. Based on the passage, which of the following statements is true?

    a. Homes with main entrances are accessible to everyone.
    b. Only some homes can be made to be more accessible.
    c. It is possible to make most homes more accessible.
    d. It takes a lot of work to make a home accessible to everyone.

2. How do wide doorways make homes more accessible?

_____

_____

_____

3. What are two ways to make a house more accessible?

_____

_____

_____

In School and at Work

1. The Americans with Disabilities Act says that people with disabilities _____

    a. have the right to get medical treatment.

    b. must live in accessible places.

    c. have the same rights to employment as everyone else.

    d. must be provided with computers in school and at work.

2. How can schools help students with disabilities?

    a. by installing wheelchair lifts and buying books in Braille

    b. by removing ramps and buying books that are easy to read

    c. by making staircases shorter and installing heavy doors

    d. all of the above

3. How can offices help workers with disabilities?

_____

_____

_____

Technology Helps

1. How can technology make homes more accessible?

    a. by making remote controls
    b. by making it easier for people to see and hear
    c. by making ramps that are easy to use
    d. by making it easier to operate machines

2. What are three examples of universal design that use technology?

_____

_____

_____

3. How is technology making universal design more common?

_____

_____

_____

disabilities	obstruction	accessible	install
Braille	audio	activated	summon

1. Choose the word from the word box above that best matches each definition. Write the word on the line below.

A. _____ of or relating to sound

B. _____ a system of writing for blind people that uses characters formed with raised dots

C. _____ something that gets in the way

D. _____ put in use; set in motion

E. _____ able to be used or reached

F. _____ to ask to come; to send for

G. _____ conditions that make people unable to do something

H. _____ to put in place

2. Fill in the blanks in the sentences below. Choose the word from the word box that completes each sentence.

A. For someone in a wheelchair, stairs can be an _____.

B. Universal design is helpful for people with _____.

C. _____ enables people who are blind to read the same books as people who can see.

D. After he fell, Mr. Watson used a special alarm system to _____ help.

E. Paul's cousin uses a wheelchair, so Paul made his house more _____.

F. The lights in my aunt's house are _____ when she claps her hands.

G. After Mom almost fell in the bathroom, we decided to _____ grab bars.

H. Mrs. Page's office has _____ controls on the phones.

Designing for All

1. Use the idea web to help you remember what you read. In each box, write the main idea of that passage.

What Is Universal Design?

_____

_____

_____

_____

At Home

_____

_____

_____

_____

Designing for All

In School and at Work

_____

_____

_____

_____

Technology Helps

_____

_____

_____

_____

2. Describe three ways universal design helps people with disabilities.

_____

_____

_____

_____

3. How does universal design help everyone, not just people with disabilities?

_____

_____

_____

_____

4. Name three examples of universal design that you have seen or heard about that are not mentioned in these passages.

_____

_____

_____

_____

Acknowledgments

Photo Credits

Cover photos: (top) BananaStock/Punchstock; (bottom, L-R) Stockbyte Silver/Getty Images; Comstock Images/Punchstock; Digital Vision/Punchstock; Dave Bartruff/Digital Vision/Getty Images; **Page:** 8 © Dana White/PhotoEdit; 10 © Bettmann/Corbis. All Rights Reserved.; 12 © Bettmann/Corbis; 14 © Bob Adelman/Magnum Photos; 22 Spike Mafford/Photodisc Green/Getty Images; 24 Silver Burdett Ginn; 26 Alberto Incrocci/The Image Bank/Getty Images; 28, 124 David Young-Wolff/Stone/Getty Images; 36 The Granger Collection, New York; 38 Atlas, copy of a Greek Hellenistic original (marble) (detail), Roman/Museo Archeologico Nazionale, Naples, Italy/The Bridgeman Art Library; 40 "Agamemnon returning from the Trojan War accompanied by Cassandra, a chariot and a Hoplite warrior," reproduction of a Greek vase (colour litho), English School (20th century)/Ancient Art and Architecture Collection Ltd., Private Collection/The Bridgeman Art Library; 42 © Jonathan Nourok/PhotoEdit; 50 Cosmo Condina/The Stock Connection; 52 © Sherri Tan/omniphoto.com. All Rights Reserved.; 54 Michael Short/Robert Harding; 56 "Pandora," 1871 (oil on canvas), Rossetti, Gabriel Charles Dante (1828-82)/Private Collection/The Bridgeman Art Library; 64, 78, 82, 84, 120, 162 © Michael Newman/PhotoEdit; 66 © Jeff Greenberg/PhotoEdit; 68 © Ron Dahlquist/SuperStock; 70 © Rhoda Sidney/PhotoEdit; 80 Merrill Education; 92 © Tony Freeman/PhotoEdit; 94 © John W. Karapelou, CMI/Phototake. All rights reserved.; 96 Custom Medical Stock Photo, Inc.; 98 Pearson Education/Prentice Hall College; 106 Brian Atkinson/Stone Allstock/Getty Images; 108 © Nik Wheeler/Corbis; 110 Emory Kristof/National Geographic Image Collection; 112 Raymond Gehman/National Geographic Image Collection; 122 Keith Brofsky/Photodisc Green/Getty Images; 126 Mikael Karisson/Arresting Images; 134 The Art Archive/National Archaeological Museum, Naples, Italy/Dagli Orti; 136 Rue des Archives/The Granger Collection, New York; 138 © Karen Preuss/The Image Works; 140 Geri Engberg Photography; 148 © Stock Market/Corbis; 150 Jane Vekshin/Photodisc Green/Getty Images; 152 © Susan Van Etten/PhotoEdit; 154 Index Stock Imagery/Punchstock; 164 Image Source/Punchstock; 166 © Peter Byron/PhotoEdit; 168 © Reuters/Corbis

Staff Credits

Members of the AMP™ QReads™ team: Melania Benzinger, Karen Blonigen, Carol Bowling, Michelle Carlson, Kazuko Collins, Nancy Condon, Barbara Drewlo, Sue Gulsvig, Daren Hastings, Laura Henrichsen, Ruby Hogen-Chin, Julie Johnston, Mary Kaye Kuzma, Julie Maas, Daniel Milowski, Carrie O'Connor, Julie Theisen, Mary Verrill, Mike Vineski, Charmaine Whitman